BRITISH GENEAL(
PERIODICALS
A
BIBLIOGRAPHY
OF THEIR CONTENTS

VOLUME 2

THE GENEALOGIST

PART 2:
FAMILY HISTORIES, PEDIGREES,
BIOGRAPHICAL NOTES, AND
OBITUARIES

— BY —

STUART RAYMOND

FEDERATION OF FAMILY HISTORY SOCIETIES

Published by the
Federation of Family History Societies,
c/o The Benson Room, Birmingham and Midland Institute,
Margaret Street, Birmingham B3 3BS, England.

Copies also obtainable from
S.A. and M.J. Raymond, 6 Russet Avenue, Heavitree, Exeter EX1 3QB, England.
S.A. and M.J. Raymond, P.O. Box 255, Belmont, Vic. 3216, Australia.

Printed by Parchment (Oxford) Limited.

Cataloguing in publication data:

Raymond Stuart A., 1945-
British genealogical periodicals: a bibliography of their contents.
Vol. 2. The Genealogist, Part 2. *Family histories, pedigrees, biographical notes, and obituaries.*
British genealogical bibliographies.
Birmingham: Federation of Family History Soceties, 1991.

DDC: 016.929

ISBN: 1 872094 31 7

ISSN: 1033-2065

INTRODUCTION

This is the second volume listing the contents of the Genealogist; a full introduction is provided in part 1. This volume lists the numerous family histories, individual pedigrees, biographical notes, and obituaries which appeared in the 44 volumes of the Genealogist between 1877 and 1921. It does not include notes and queries, except where they provide substantial information, or refer to previously published articles. In the latter case, volume, year & page numbers only are cited in a 'see also' reference after the main article.

Collections of pedigrees are listed in part 1, as are works on the descent of titles, and a wide variety of other source material. This work should be used in conjunction with the name indexes to be found in each volume of the Genealogist, and in:

An index of subjects contained in the Genealogist (New series), vols. 1-XX. Exeter: W. Pollard, 1905. Supplement to N.S., 20.

The Genealogist is available in many British libraries, and in research libraries throughout the English-speaking world. Your local librarian should be able to advise you where it may be consulted. I am grateful to the librarians of Devon County Library, the Devon and Exeter Institution, and the State Library of Victoria, in Melbourne, Australia, for access to their runs of the journal. I am also grateful to Brian Christmas for his assistance in proof-reading.

This work is designed to be used in conjunction with my English genealogy: an introductory bibliography, and the other works in the British genealogical bibliographies series. Further particulars of the series are printed on the back cover.

Stuart A. Raymond

FAMILY HISTORIES, PEDIGREES, BIOGRAPHICAL NOTES, AND OBITUARIES

ABERNETHY

WALLACE-JAMES, J. G. 'The Abernethy family', N.S., 17, 1901, p.150-2. See also N.S., 18, 1902, p.16-25, 73-8, & 208. Scotland; 13-17th c.

ADELIZA

ROUND, J. H. 'Adeliza, the Viscountess', N.S., 5, 1892, p.148-50. Continues debate concerning Lincoln family, q.v.

ALDER

See Smart

ALLEN

ALLEN, W. C. Hanwell. 'Extracts from the parish registers of Thurcoston, Co. Leicester, relating to the family of Allen', 5, 1881, p.131-2.

RYLANDS, J. Paul. 'A pedigree of the family of Allen, of Chester and of Brindley, Co. Chester', N.S., 34, 1918, p.147-8. 16-17th c.

ALLESTRY

PINK, W. D. 'Allestry, of Alvaston, Co. Derby', N.S., 32, 1916, p.164-71. 16-19th c; includes wills.

ALLEYN

RENDLE, William. 'Edward Alleyn', N.S., 2, 1884, p.241-55. London; 16th c.

AMES

AMES, Reginald. 'Pedigree of Ames', 2, 1878, p.273-81. Somerset, Gloucestershire, Hertfordshire & London; 17-19th c.

'In memoriam: Reginald Ames', N.S., 8, 1892, p.185.

AMYAS

'From the register of Great Dunham, Norfolk', 2, 1878, p.130-1. See also p.271. Amias family, 17th c; Includes extracts from parish registers of Little Dunham & Lutcham alias Litcham, and wills.

ANDERSON

'Pedigree of Anderson and Timins', 5, 1881, p.205-7. 19th c.

ANGUS

See Umframville

ANNESLEY

B., B. H. 'Annesley and Bourke families', 3, 1879, p.18. Extracts from family bible, 17-18th c.

ARNOLD

See Sargent

ARUNDEL

BOND, T. 'Remarks on Mr. Pym Yeatman's notice of the barony of Roger Arundel in his History of the house of Arundel. N.S., 1, 1884, p.97-102 & 157-69.

'The house of Arundel', 7, 1883, p.65-70. Review article on Pym Yeatman's The house of Arundel. See also Yeatman's reply, p.190-1.

ASHMOLE

SMITH, J. Challenor. 'Elias Ashmole's second wife', N.S., 29, 1913, p.86-7. Marriages of Mary Forster to Stafford, Hamlyn, Mainwaring & Ashmole; 17th c.

ASHTON

GREEN, Everard. 'Pedigree of the family of Ashton of Spalding and Grantham, Co. Lincoln', 2, 1878, p.327-31. 15-18th c.

ASPINWALL

ASPINALL, H. O. 'The Aspinwall and Aspinall families of Lancashire', N.S., 32, 1916, p.145-53 & 233-45; 33, 1917, p.16-27, 81-93, 162-77 & 240-60; 34, 1918, p.9-28, 88-102, 134-47 & 190-206; 35, 1919, p.25-35, 138-61 & 203-15; 36, 1920, p.22-40, 83-92, 138-53 & 183-97; 37, 1921, p.46-50, 84-94, 154-62 & 196-210. Incomplete; includes pedigrees, 13-19th c.

ASSHETON

BEATTY, Joseph M. 'Sir Robert de Assheton, treasurer of England', N.S., 36, 1920, p.62-70. Lancashire; 14th c.

ATSLOW

CHURCH, A. H. 'The family of Atslow', N.S., 21, 1905, p.60-63. Essex; 16-18th c.

AUDLEY

CHAPIN, Howard M. 'The identity of Saint Catherine Audley', N.S., 30, 1914, p.190-1. Herefordshire; 14th c.

DRAKE, William R. 'Note as to the parentage of Blanche Audley, the wife of Robert Hatch of Wolley, Co. Devon', 4, 1880; p.69-75. Includes pedigree of Audley, 14th c.

See also De Braose

BADGERS

See Pointer

BALLIOL

BAIN, Joseph. 'The Baliol le Scot family and their heart stone', N.S., 15, 1899, p.11. Legend concerning Kentish connections.

BAIN, Joseph. 'Sir Alexander Balliol of Cavers (Chamberlain of Scotland)' N.S., 4, 1887, p.141-3. Roxburghshire.

VINCENT, John A. C. 'Sir Alexander Balliol of Cavers, and the barony of Valoynes', 6, 1882, p.1-7. Roxburghshire; 13th c.

BARIL

See Berchere

BARKER

ROUND, J. H. 'Pedigree of Barker', N.S., 11, 1895, p.65-7. Suffolk; 17th c.

BARNOUIN

WAGNER, Henry. 'The Huguenot refugee family of Barnouin', N.S., 25, 1909, p.44-5. 18-19th c.

BARROW

CRAWLEY-BOEVEY, Arthur William 'Pedigree of Sir Charles Barrow, Bart., of High-Grove, Minsterworth, Co. Gloucester', N.S., 30, 1914, p.73-86. 16-18th c., includes wills.

BEAUCHAMP

CARTER, W. F. 'The Beauchamps of Somerset', N.S., 33, 1917, p.151-4. 11-14th c.

See also Mandeville

BEAUMONT

WHITE, G. H. 'Robert de Beaumont and the Comte of Meulan', N.S., 36, 1920, p.173-8. 11th c.

BECKETT

RICHARDSON, W. H. 'Beckett entries from the register of Brailes, Co. Warwick', 2, 1878, p.30-31.

BEDINGFELD

KENNEDY, Arthur J. Clark. 'Bedingfeld: from the parish registers of Darsham, Suffolk', 2, 1878, p.29.

WADLEY, T. P. 'Bedingfeld, from the parish registers of Ditchingham, Norfolk', 1, 1877, p.239-40. 17-18th c.

BEESTON

'Pedigree of the very ancient family of the Beestons of Beeston', 1, 1877, p.175-6. Yorkshire; 13-16th c.

BELHAVEN

GIBBS, Vicary. 'The first Lord Belhaven and Stenton', N.S., 20, 1904, p.77-8. Scotland; 17th c.

BENINGWORTH

B., W. H. B. 'Beningworth of Beningworth', N.S., 15, 1899, p.12-16. See also p.68-70 & 140-45. Lincolnshire; includes pedigree, 12-14th c.

POYNTON, E. M. 'The heirs of William Fitz Ralph and the family of Beningworth', N.S., 17, 1901, p.82-9. Lincolnshire; 12-13th c.

BENNETT

COKAYNE, G. E. 'Diary of Alexander Bennett, 1705 to 1758', N.S., 20, 1904, p.145-54. London; of the East India Company.

KING, Edward. 'Bennett of Hexworthy in the parish of Lawhitton and county of Cornwall', 4, 1880, p.144-50.

'Pedigree of Bennett', N.S., 20, 1904, p.238-49. London; 17-18th c; includes pedigree of Merttins 18th c.

BENTINCK

ROUND, J. H. 'William Bentinck, first Earl of Portland', N.S., 18, 1902, p.36-7.

BERCHERE

WAGNER, Henry. 'Pedigree of the Huguenot refugee families of Berchere and Baril', N.S., 23, 1907, p.248-51. London; 17-18th c.

BERINGTON

See Whittingham

BERKELEY

BARKLY, Sir Henry. 'The earliest pipe roll', N.S., 3, 1886, p.79. Gloucestershire; Berkeley family, 11th c.

BERRY

See Levett

BERTIE

See Bland

BICKLEY

BICKLEY, W. B. 'A descendant of Sir William Dugdale', N.S., 29, 1913, p.49. Pedigree of Bickley, of Halloughton, Warwickshire; 17-18th c; includes monumental inscriptions.

BLACKER

B., B. H. 'Blacker family', 3, 1879, p.54-5. Ireland; 18th c.

BLAND

COKAYNE, G. E. 'Bland, of Carleton, Co. York, as connected with the family of Cary, Willoughby and Bertie', N.S., 23, 1907, p.201-6. 17-18th c.

BLAQUIERE

See De Varenne

BLOUNT

NOBLE, Mark. 'History of the beautiful Elizabeth Blount', 2, 1878, p.19-24 & 44-52. 16th c. Includes pedigree of Talboys, 15-17th c.

BOHUN

WATSON, G. W. 'The Bohuns of Midhurst', N.S., 28, 1912, p.1-16, 114-23 & 173-4. Sussex; 11-16th c.

See also De Braose

BOISSIER

WAGNER, Henry. 'Pedigree of the protestant refugee families of Boissier, Sellon, and De Villettes', 6, 1882, p.168-76. Geneva; 18-19th c.

BOOTH

SYKES, John. 'Booth family: addition to Le Neve's knights', N.S., 3, 1886, p.135.

BORLASE

See Taillefer

BOUCHIER

BOUCHER, R. 'Notes on the family of Elizabeth (Bouchier), wife of the Protector, Oliver Cromwell', N.S., 28, 1912, p.65-75. 16-17th c; includes wills.

BOWDLER

GYLL, Gordon. 'Notes on the surname of Bowdler', 1, 1877, p.279-84. See also p.390-3, & 2, 1878, p.30. Includes pedigree, lists of wills, & parish register extracts.

BOX

ELLIS, W. S. 'Notes on the family of Box', 1, 1877, p.97-100. Kent & Sussex; includes wills, extracts from parish registers, etc.

BOYVILLE

WAGNER, Henry. 'Pedigree of the descendants of Peter de Boyville', N.S., 36, 1920, p.124-5. 18th c; includes Payne family.

BOURKE

See Annesley

BRADFORD

'Pedigree of Bradford', 5, 1887, p.293-5. Northumberland; medieval.

BRADSHAW

See Urmston

BRECHIN

BAIN, Joseph. 'Sir David of Brechin, executed in 1320', N.S., 5, 1888, p.22-5. Forfarshire.

BROOKE

HARWOOD, H. W. Forsyth. 'The true descent of Brooke of Astley', N.S., 13, 1897, p.222-8. Lancashire; 17-18th c., includes wills.

BROWNE

C., A. C. 'Thomas Browne, Garter King of Arms, 1774-1780, 36, 1920, p. v-vi.

LARKEN, Arthur Staunton, & GREEN, Everard. 'Pedigree of the family of Browne of Horbling, Co. Lincoln', 3, 1879, p.70-77. See also p.191-2, & 5, 1881, p.113. 16-19th c.

[MARSHALL, G. W.] 'Sir Richard Browne, Kt., and Bart.', 3, 1879, p.377-9. See also 4, 1880, p.128-9, & 5, 1881, p.185.

BRUCE

ARMSTRONG, W. Bruce. 'Bruces of Cultmalundie in Perthshire, of Muness, of Sumburgh, of Symbister in Shetland', 6, 1882, p.162-7 & 205-11. 15-18th c.

'An account of the Bruces of Newtoune, and the Irish branch descended of that house and now representing it in the male line', 3, 1879, p.19-26 & 38-46. Scotland & Ireland; 17-19th c.

'Bruce of Earlshall in the parish of Leuchars, Co. Fife', 7, 1883, p.131-42. 15-19th c.

BUCCLEUCH

NAPIER, Mark. 'Tradition: the Thirlestane murder; a pendant to the Wigtown martyrdom', 1, 1877, p.194-201. Thirlestane, Berwickshire.

BUCHAN

See Comyn and Van Borssele

BUCKBY

See Osborne

BUCKLE

RICE, Robert Garroway. 'The Buckles of Banstead, Co. Surrey', 3, 1879, p.251-8. Includes extracts from parish registers, 17-19th c.

BURDEN

S. 'Burden of Auckengarrick and Feddall, Co. Perth', 3, 1879, p.145-50.

BURGH

C[OKAYNE], G. E. 'Pedigree of the Lords Burgh of Gainsborough', N.S., 12, 1896, p.233-5. Lincolnshire; 15-17th c.

BURKE

'In memoriam: Sir Bernard Burke', N.S., 9, 1893, p.186.

BURNETT

PAUL, J. Balfour. 'In memoriam: George Burnett, esq., LL.D., advocate, Lyon King of Arms', N.S., 6, 1890, p.213-5.

BUTLER

HALL, Hamilton. 'Note on the family of Butler, afterwards Earls of Ormonde', N.S. 25, 1909, p.73-8. Ireland; 13-14th c.

See also Ormonde

BYNES

RENSHAW, Walter C. 'The Bynes of Carshalton, Co. Surrey', N.S., 23, 1907, p.213-9. 17-19th c.

RENSHAW, Walter C. 'The Bynes of Rowdell in Washington, Co. Sussex', N.S., 23, 1907, p.1-11. 16-18th c.

CAMPBELL

CAMPBELL, Herbert. 'Campbell Earl of Loudon: some notes on the peerage contained in The Scots peerage, vol. 5', N.S., 37, 1921, p.183-91.

'Campbell of Lawers, Co. Perth', 5, 1881, p.132-7. See also p.298-9.

CAMPBELL, Herbert. 'The Campbells of Duntroon', N.S., 27, 1911, p.193-200. Argyll; 15-17th c.

CAMPBELL, Herbert. 'The Campbells of Ellanrie and the Campbells of Rudill (both cadets of Duntroon)', N.S., 29, 1913, p.22-30. Argyll; 16-18th c.

CAMPBELL, Herbert. 'The Campbells of Larigs and Stronmialachan (tacksmen)', N.S., 31, 1915, p.153-9. See also p.284. Argyll; 18-19th c.

CAMPBELL, Herbert. 'The Campbells of Lergnachunzeon (cadets of Duntroon)', N.S., 28, 1912, p.199-208. Argyll; 16-19th c.

CAMPBELL, Herbert. 'The Campbells of Oib', N.S., 28, 1912, p.24-34. Argyll; 16-18th c.

CAMPBELL, Herbert. 'The Campbells of Raschoille', N.S., 28, 1912, p.100-108 & 142-9. Argyll; 17-18th c.

CAMPBELL, Herbert. 'The Campbells of Skeldoun, cadets of Loudon', N.S., 27, 1911, p.154-7. Ayrshire; 16th c.

CAMPBELL, Herbert. 'Extracts from a Campbell bible', N.S., 31, 1915, p.44-6. Scotland; 18th c.

CAMPBELL, Herbert. 'Duntroon papers', N.S., 34, 1918, p.65-73, 126-33 & 210-18; 35, 1919, p.35-44, 178-84, & 226-35; 36, 1920, p.40-42 & 204-15. Campbell family papers, 17-18th c.

CAMPBELL, Herbert. 'Further notes on the Campbells of Duntroon', N.S., 31, 1915, p.239-43; 32, 1916, p.20-30 & 91-101. Argyll; 15-18th c.

CAMPBELL, Herbert. 'Further notes on the Campbells of Duntroon: amendments and additions', N.S., 37, 1921, p.33-46 & 66-73. Includes pedigrees, 15-18th c.

CAMPBELL, Herbert. 'A note on the origin of Campbell of Duntroon', N.S., 27, 1911, p.27-8. Argyll; 14th c.

CAMPBELL, Herbert. 'Some notes on the two Campbell families of Ardlarich and Ardtarich', N.S., 29, 1913, p.209-12. Argyll.

CAMPBELL, Herbert. 'Some other cadets of Duntroon: Culva, Krap and Torobolls' N.S., 29, 1913, p.71-8. Argyll; 17-18th c.

CAMPBELL, Herbert. 'Some other writs relating to the Campbells of Duntroon', N.S., 36, 1920, p.77-82. Argyll; 16-18th c.

CANNING

WADLEY, T. P. 'The Cannings of Foxcott', 4, 1880, p.157-65. Foxcott, Warwickshire, and Gloucestershire; includes extracts from parish registers.

CAREW

GLENCROSS, Reginald M. 'The Carews, Baronets of Antony, Co. Cornwall', N.S., 2, 1908, p.22-5. See also 25, 1909, p.154-6. 17-18th c.

CARMICHAEL

G. 'Carmichael family', N.S., 2, 1885, p.15. See also p.240 & 3, 1886, p.188. Of Dungannon, Ireland.

CARRE

C. 'Carre of Sleaford and Carr of Stackhouse', 3, 1879, p.380-6. Lincolnshire & Yorkshire; 15-17th c.

C. 'Family of Carre or Carr of Sleaford', 3, 1879, p.193-206. See also 4, 1880, p.169. Lincolnshire; 16-17th c.

'Carre of Cavers-Carre, County of Roxburgh', 3, 1879, p.110-15. 16-18th c.

See also Kerr and Smart

CARRIBER

WALLACE-JAMES, J. G. 'The feudal casualty of marriage', N.S., 16, 1900, p.27-8. Hadingtonshire; notarial instrument concerning the refusal of Katherine Carriber of 'Quhitkirk' to marry at the command of her feudal superior, 1589.

CARY

See Bland

CASTELION

EARWAKER, J. P. 'Pedigree of Castelion', 6, 1882, p.136-8. Berkshire; 16-17th c.

COKAYNE, G. E. 'Pedigree of Castillion', N.S., 17, 1901, p.73-82, 199-204 & 225-32. 16-17th c; includes extracts from parish registers, wills, monumental inscriptions, etc.

CHALIE

WAGNER, Henry. 'Pedigree of the Huguenot refugee (now extinct) family of Chalie', N.S., 19, 1903, p.59-61. London; 18-19th c.

CHAMBERLAIN

See Osbert

CHAPMAN

MURRAY, Keith W. 'Chapman of Hertfordshire and London', N.S., 34, 1918, p.1-5. 16-17th c.

CHARDIN

WAGNER, Henry. 'Pedigree of Chardin', N.S., 31, 1915, p.96-8. 17-18th c.

CHESNEY

See Stewart

CHESTER

FLETCHER, W. G. D. 'The Chesters of Chicheley: some additions and corrections', N.S., 25, 1909, p.145-53. Leicestershire, 18th c; includes wills.

MARSHALL, George W. 'Joseph Lemuel Chester, D.C.L.', 6, 1882, p.189-92. Obituary.

CHOWNE

RENSHAW, Walter C. 'The Chownes of Alfriston, Co. Sussex', N.S., 24, 1908, p.73-80. 16-18th c.

CHURCH

CHURCH, A. H. 'Percy Church: a forgotten royalist', N.S., 13, 1897, p.214-22. See also 14, 1898, p.84-5, & 280.

CLARKE

RICHARDSON, W. H. 'Pedigree of the family of Clarke of Yarnscombe, Co. Devon, and of Waste Court, Abingdon, Co. Berks; from the records of the College of Arms', 2, 1878, p.169-75. 18-19th c; includes grant of arms, 1876, and extracts from Yarnscombe, Holsworthy and Great Torrington, Devon, parish registers.

CLARMONT

WAGNER, Henry. 'Pedigree of the Huguenot family of Clarmont', N.S., 26, 1910, p.160-1. 18th c.

CLAYTON

FLETCHER, W. G. D. 'The family of Clayton, of Great Grimsby, Co. Lincoln', N.S., 23, 1907, p.80-83. 16-18th c.

CLAYTON

'The pedigree of the Claytons of Crooke, Fulwood, and Adlington, in the county of Lancaster', N.S., 26, 1910, p.129-42. 16-19th c.

CLERE

JESSOP, Augustus. 'Pedigree of Clere of Blickling', 3, 1879, p.291-4. Norfolk; 16-17th c., includes extracts from parish registers.

RYE, Walter. 'Doubtful Norfolk Pedigree, No. IV, Clere', 4, 1880, p.99-102. 11-14th c.

CODRINGTON

See Isaac

COKAYNE

LEE, G. Ambrose. 'The late Clarenceaux King of Arms', N.S., 28, 1912, p.150-51. Obituary of George Edward Cokayne.

COLE

'Cole of Co. Cork', 3, 1879, p.289-91. 18-19th c.

COMBRUNE

WAGNER, Henry. 'The Huguenot refugee family of Combrune', N.S., 24, 1908, p.194-5. London; 18th c.

COMYN

BAIN, Joseph. 'The Earldom of Buchan', N.S., 4, 1887, p.194-6. 14th c., Comyn family.

CONINGSBY

BELLEWES, G. O. 'The two Coningsbys, justices of the Kings Bench', N.S., 26, 1910, p.212-7. 16th c., includes wills.

COOPER

KEMEYS-TYNTE, St. David M. 'Baronetcy of Cooper of Gogar', N.S., 24, 1908, p.89-96. Midlothian; 17-19th c. See also p.216.

S. 'Cooper of Gogar', 1, 1877, p.257-66. See also p.334. Midlothian; 13-19th c.

COPLEY

SANBORN, V. C. 'The Copleys of Roughey and Gatton', N.S., 33, 1917, p.73-80. Roughey, Sussex, and Gatton, Surrey; includes 15-16th c. pedigrees.

CORBOULD

ROUND, J. Horace. 'Corbould family', N.S., 2, 1885, p.94-5. Suffolk; includes pedigree, 17th c.

CORNEWALL

MARSHALL, G. W. 'The Barons of Burford, No.11'. 4, 1886, p. 76-86. Shropshire; Cornewall family, 16-18th c.

CORNWALL

COOKE, J. H. 'Isobel de Cornwall', 3, 1879, p.294-5. 13th c.

[MARSHALL, G. W.] 'The Barons of Burford', 3, 1879, p.225-30. Cornwall family; Shropshire; 13-16th c.

COTTIN

MURRAY, Keith W. 'Genealogy of the family of Cottin, settled in England from St. Quentin, in France', N.S., 23, 1907, p. 207-12; 24, 1908, p.81-8.

COUCY

'Ingelram de Coucy, Earl of Bedford', N.S., 4, 1887, p.89-91. See also p.172. 14th c.

COURTENAY

BAIN, Joseph. 'Some notes on William de Courtenay, founder of Worspring Priory, his wife Ada of Dunbar, and his probable place in the Courtenay pedigree', N.S., 3, 1886, p.193-7. Berwickshire; 12th c.

'The runaway match of Elizabeth Courtenay', 6, 1882, p.193-9. Devon; includes pedigree, 15th c.

COWELL

CLAY, C. T. 'An eighteenth century Quakeress of Leeds, with some account of the family of Cowell', N.S., 36, 1920, p.178-82. Yorkshire; 17-18th c.

CRADOCK

FLETCHER, W. G. Dimock. 'Cradock of Loughborough, Co. Leicester', 6, 1882, p.19-23. See also 7, 1883, p.24. 18-19th c.

CREFFIELD

ROUND, J. H. 'The Creffield family', N.S., 3, 1898, p.80-83. London & Surrey; includes 18th c. pedigree.

CREON

POYNTON, E. M. 'The fee of Creon', N.S., 18, 1902, p.162-6 & 219-25. Lincolnshire; 12-13th c.

CREUZE

WAGNER, Henry. 'A tentative pedigree of the (now extinct) Huguenot refugee family of Creuze', N.S., 27, 1911, p.114-5. London; 18th c.

CREWE

CARTER, William F. 'The early Crewe pedigree', N.S., 37, 1921, p.113-27 & 174-83. Cheshire; medieval.

CROMWELL

ROUND, J. H. 'Oliver Cromwell and his "Stuart" descent', N.S., 10, 1894, p.18-19. 16th c.

RYE, Walter. 'Oliver Cromwell's descent from the Steward family', N.S., 1, 1884, p.150-7.

RYE, Walter. 'The Steward genealogy and Cromwell's "royal" descent', N.S., 2, 1885, p.34-42.

See also Bouchier

CRUSO

BARNARD, George W. G. 'Pedigree of the family of Cruso', N.S., 18, 1902, p.246-52. Norfolk and various other counties; 17-19th c.

CUMMING

TOMKINS, H. Barr. 'Sir Kenneth William Cumming of Culter, Baronet', 3, 1879, p.1-12. Lanarkshire; 17-19th c.

D'ABZAC

WAGNER, Henry. 'Pedigree of D'Abzac', N.S., 18, 1902, p.57-9. 17-19th c. France & Dublin.

DALE

See Levett

DALLAS

DALLAS, James. 'Dallas of Budzet, or Budgate', 4, 1880. p.121-3. Invernessshire. 13-17th C.

DALLAS, James. 'Entries on the fly-leaf of a bible, formerly belonging to Lachlan Dallas', 3, 1879, p.406-7. Scotland; 18th c.

DANVERS

'From the registers of Swithland, Co. Leicr', 1, 1877, p.5. Danvers family burials, 17-18th c.

DANYERS

RYLANDS, J. Paul. 'A vellum pedigree-roll of the family of Danyers alias Danyell, of the county of Chester', N.S., 32, 1916, p.7-19. 13-17th c.

DARASSUS

WAGNER, Henry. 'Descendants of Jean Darassus', N.S., 34, 1918, p.42-3. Ireland; 18th c.

DAUBENEY

GAIRDNER, James, & ROUND, J. H. 'The barony of Daubeney', N.S., 4, 1887, p.42-6. 14th c.

DAVALL

BERTHON, Raymond Tinne. 'The family of Peter Davall, F.R.S., Master in Chancery', N.S., 31, 1915, p.223-38. London & Essex; 17-18th c. Includes wills.

DAVYS

FLETCHER, W. G. Dimock. 'Pedigree of Davys, of Tisbury, Co. Wilts., of Rempstone, Co. Nottingham; and of Castle Donington and Loughborough, Co. Leicester', 5, 1881, p.25-32. 16-19th c.

DE BRAOSE

DRAKE, Sir William R. 'Note on the De Braose, Martyn, Audley and Fitzwaryn pedigrees', 6, 1882, p.16-19. Devon; includes pedigree, 14-15th c.

ELWES, D. G. C. 'De Braose', 5, 1881, p.147. Includes pedigree, 13th c.

ELWES, Dudley G. Cary. 'De Braose Family', 4, 1880, p.133-41 & 235-44; 5, 1881, p.65-70, 161-7 & 318-25; 6, 1882, p.236-47; 7, 1883, p.51-60. Medieval; includes pedigree of Bohun of Midhurst, Sussex.

DE BRETTES

Gaury, F. H. H. 'Pedigree of De Brettes and De Loudeix', N.S., 11, 1895, p.172-3. France; 16-18th c.

DE CLARE

RYE, Walter. 'The De Clares of Clare in Suffolk (Earls of Gloucester) and the De Cleres of Ormesby and Stokesby in Norfolk', N.S., 37, 1921, p.169-73. 12-13th c.

DE COPPET

See Kinloch

DE LA POLE

ROUND, J. H. 'Note on the De La Pole pedigree', N.S., 3, 1886, p.112.

DE LOUDEIX

See De Brettes

DE MAINBRAY

WAGNER, Henry. 'Pedigree of De Mainbray, N.S., 27, 1911, p.22-3. London; 18th c.

DE MORAVIA

See Moray

DENBIGH

See Feilding

DENTON

WELBY, Alfred C. E. 'A fifteenth century abduction', N.S., 23, 1907, p.83-8. Denton family.

DERBY

See Stanley

DE RHAM

See Kinloch

DESAGULIERS

WAGNER, Henry. 'Descendants of Jean Desaguliers (Huguenot refugee)', 5, 1881, p.117-22.

DE ST. WALERY

FOWLER, G. Herbert. 'De St. Walery', N.S., 30, 1914, p.1-17. Ponthieu and England; includes pedigree, 10-13th c.

DE SAY

See Fitzpiers

DESBOROUGH

HOLWORTHY, F. M. R. 'Particulars relating to the family of Desborough, copied from a Desborough family bible', N.S., 26, 1910, p.147-8. Huntingdonshire, etc., 18th c.

DE VARENNE

WAGNER, Henry. 'The Huguenot refugee family of De Varenne', N.S., 23, 1907, p.62-3. 17-18th c. Female descent through Blaquiere & Savary.

DEVAYNES

WAGNER, Henry. 'The Huguenot family of Devaynes', N.S., 21, 1905, p.202-3. 18-19th c.

DE VILLETTES

See Boissier

DEYNCOURT

B., W. H. B. 'The Kirkstead chartulary: Deyncourt', N.S., 17, 1901, p.161-3. Lincolnshire; Deyncourt family pedigree, 12-14th c.

DIMOCK

FLETCHER, W. G. Dimock. 'Dimock Family', 4, 1880, p.98-9. 19th c. extracts from Upping Lane, Rutland, parish register.

FLETCHER, W. G. Dimock. 'Dimock of Randwick and Stonehouse, Co. Gloucester', 2, 1878, p.181-3. See also 3, 1879, p.326-7. 18-19th c.

FLETCHER, W. G. Dimock. 'Register extracts relating to Dimock family', 2, 1878, p.213-4. From Randwick, Gloucestershire, 17-18th c.

DOBSON

JOYCE, G. Haywood. 'Dobson and Fell families', N.S., 3, 1886, p.145-7. Mainly Hampshire; 17-18th c.

DODD

See Portales

DODINGTON

'Pedigree of Dodington, from visitation of Somerset, 1623', 1, 1877, p.23-9. See also p.155-6. 14-17th c., includes 16-17th c. extracts from Dodington parish register.

See also Marriott-Dodington

D'OILLI

ROUND, J. H. 'Notes on the pedigree of D'Oilli', N.S., 5, 1888, p.80-1. 13th c.

DONEGAL

See Williams

DOUGLAS

'Pedigree of Douglas of Tilquhilly, or Tilwhilly, Co. Kincardine', 5, 1881, p.193-204. 16-19th c.

DRAKE

DRAKE, H. H. 'Drake and his detractors', N.S., 2, 1885, p.275-9.

DUDINGSTOUN

MURRAY, K. W. 'Genealogy of Dudingstoun of Southouse, 1335-1600', N.S., 15, 1899, p.7-10. See also 17, 1901, p.288. Midlothian.

DUFF

CRAMOND, Wm. 'The Earl of Fife', N.S., 3, 1886, p.205-10. See also p. 256. Scotland; Duff family, 17th c.

DUGDALE

'Dugdale', 4, 1880, p.124-5. Extracts from parish registers of St. Lawrence Jewry, London, etc., 18th c.

See also Bickley

DUKINFIELD

RYLANDS, J. Paul. 'A vellum pedigree of the families of Dukinfield, Co. Chester, and Holland, of Denton, Co. Lancaster, drawn in the year 1622', N.S., 32, 1916, p.85-90. 13-17th c.

DU MOULIN-BROWNE

C., I. M. 'Du Moulin-Browne of Easebourne, and Moore of Fawley', N.S., 8, 1892, p.30-33. Easebourne, Sussex, and Fawley, ? Hampshire; 18-19th c.

DUPPA

SMITH, J. Challenor. 'Bishop Duppa's wife', N.S., 4, 1887, p.116-8. Includes pedigree of Mallory, Killingtree & Marsh, 17th c.

DUPRAT DE CHARREAU

WAGNER, Henry. 'A study of the Huguenot refugee families of Duprat de Charreau, and Maseres', N.S., 24, 1908, p.264-5. London; 18th c.

DWIGHT

CHURCH, Sir Arthur H. 'The family of John Dwight, B.C.L., potter', N.S., 27, 1911, p.74-77. London; includes pedigree, 15-18th c.

DWNN

LAW, W. T. 'Lewis Dwnn's patent as deputy herald', N.S., 19, 1903, p.233-4. 1585.

EDWARDS

ROUND, J. H. 'Pedigree of Edwards (London visitation of 1634)', N.S., 10, 1894, p.183-5. 17-18th c.

ELIOT

MORRIS, George J. 'The ravishment of Sir John Eliot's son', N.S., 1, 1884, p.21-6.

ELLIS

ELLIS, A. S. 'In memoriam: William Smith Ellis, esq.', N.S., 7, 1891, p.34-6.

EU

See Mauclerk

EVINGTON

GREEN, Everard. 'Pedigree of Evington of Spalding, Co. Lincoln', 2, 1878, p.263-5.

EXELBY

ESHELBY, H. D. 'Notes on the genealogy of Exelby of London, Herts. &c', N.S., 10, 1894, p.20-28, 116-22 & 146-55. Includes pedigree, 16-19th c.

FAIRFAX

WADDINGTON, G. W. 'The Fairfax family: extracts from the parish registers of Whitby, Co. York', 2, 1878, p.390.

FALKENER

See Le Fauconer

FANE

FANE, W. V. R. 'The pedigree of the Fane and Vane family', N.S., 13, 1897, p.81-6. See also p.209-13, & 14. 1898, p.71-2. Kent; 1450-1600.

FASCHIN

C., F. T. 'Faschin family', 7, 1883, p.236. See also N.S., 1, 1884, p.32. Of Guernsey.

FAWKENER

See Le Fauconer

FAZAKERLEY

See Hawarden

FEILDING

ROUND, J. H. 'Our English Hapsburgs: a great delusion', N.S., 10, 1894, p.193-206. Feilding family, Earls of Denbigh; medieval.

FELL

See Dobson

FERBY

BELLEWES, G. O. 'The Ferbys of Paul's Cray Hill, Kent; N.S., 27, 1911, p.8-14. 15-17th c.

FERRAR

RYLANDS, J. Paul. 'Some memorials of the family of Ferrar, of Little Gidding, Co. Huntingdon', N.S., 26, 1910, p.65-72. Includes pedigree, 16-18th c., with memorial inscriptions.

FERRERS

FERRERS, Cecil S. F. 'Pedigree of the Berkshire and London branch of the Ferrers family, as compiled by Sir Edward Wilson, Bart., (1752), Edmund Ferrers, F.S.A., rector of Cheriton, Hants (1806-1825) and other later members of the family', N.S, 27, 1911, p.24-6. London; 17-19th c.

FIELD

FLETCHER, W. G. Dimock. 'Field, of Laceby and Ulceby, Co. Lincoln', 2, 1878, p.344-7; 5, 1881, p.179-83, & N.S., 1, 1884, p.92-6. 17-19th c., includes extracts from parish registers, wills, inquisitions post mortem, & monumental inscriptions.

FISHBORNE

'Fishborne', 5, 1881, p.323. 17th c.

FITZ GEOFFREY

See Mandeville

FITZGILBERT

BAIN, Joseph. 'Walter Fitz Gilbert, ancestor of the Dukes of Hamilton', N.S., 2, 1885, p.43-6. 13-14th c.

FITZPIERS

WATSON, G. W. 'Fitz Piers and De Say', N.S., 34, 1918, p.181-9. Hampshire; includes pedigrees, 12-13th c., and deeds.

FITZRALPH

See Beningworth

FITZROY

TURNER, G. J. 'Richard Fitzroy', N.S., 22, 1906, p.105-10. 13th c.

FITZWARYN

See De Braose and Grove

FLEETWOOD

BEWLEY, Sir Edmund T. 'An Irish branch of the Fleetwood family', N.S., 24, 1908, p.217-41. Includes pedigrees, 16-19th c.

BEWLEY, Sir Edmund T. 'A further note on an Irish branch of the Fleetwood family', N.S., 25, 1909, p.21-2.

FLEMING

BAIN, Joseph. 'Henry II of France and the Dowager Lady Fleming', N.S., 10, 1894, p.17-18. Scotland; 16th c.

See also Stewart

FOLEY

GRAZEBROOK, H. Sydney. 'The origin of the Foley family', 6, 1881, p.117-22. Worcestershire; 17th c.

FOLLIOTT

BEWLEY, Edmund T. 'The Folliotts of Londonderry and Chester', N.S., 20, 1904, p.108-13. 17-19th c.

FORSETT

SMITH, G. C. Moore. 'Forsett of Marylebone and Wells Hall, Co. Suffolk', N.S., 21, 1905, p.106-13. Marylebone, Middlesex; pedigree, 16-17th c.

FORSTER

FLETCHER, W. G. D. 'License to John Forster to wear his bonnet in the royal presence, 1520', N.S., 18, 1902, p.218-9. Shropshire.

See also Ashmole

FORTESCUE

WADLEY, Thomas P. 'Fortescue of Cookhill, Co. Worcester', 3, 1879, p.115-8. Includes monumental inscriptions and parish register extracts.

FOWLER

CARTER, William F. 'The Fowlers of Hambleton', 7, 18 & 3, p.4-10. Hambleton, Rutland; also of Oxfordshire, Bedforshire & Buckinghamshire. Includes wills, 16-17th c.

FOX

SMITH, J. Challenor. 'The families of Fox and Tattershall', N.S., 30, 1912, p.150-3. Middlesex and Hampshire; 16th c.

FREIND

JEWERS, Arthur J. 'Pedigree of the family of Freind, with monumental inscriptions, abstracts of wills, and other evidences', N.S., 30, 1914, p.230-38; 31, 1915, p.34-44. 17-19th c., includes pedigree of Morice, 17-19th c.

GALE

SMITH, J. C. C. 'New notes on the ancestry of George Washington', 7, 1883, p.1-3. Primarily concerned with Gale of Whitehaven, Cumberland; includes 18th c. pedigree of Gale.

GALHIE

WAGNER, Henry. 'The Huguenot refugee family of Galhie', N.S., 28, 1912, p.216-7. London; 18th c.

GALLOWAY

See Stewart

GALLY

WAGNER, Henry. 'Huguenot refugee family of Gally', N.S., 25, 1909, p.93. 18-19th c.

GAMLYN

GREEN, Everard. 'Pedigree of Gamlyn of Spalding, Co. Lincoln', 2, 1877, p.386-7. 16-18th c.

GARNHAM

B., W. H. B. 'Pedigree of Garnham, continued from the visitation of Berkshire in 1664', N.S., 16, 1900, p.96-7. 17-18th c.

GAURY

'Pedigree of the Gaury and Mourier de Lalande families', N.S., 9, 1893, p.183-5. France; 18-19th c.

GELLIBRAND

See Hawarden

GENEVA

See Lacy

GERARD

RYLANDS, J. Paul. 'A pedigree of the family of Gerard of Crewood, Frodsham, &c., in the county of Chester, drawn by Randle Holme of Chester in 1691, and the descent continued in the family of Perryn of Trafford Hall in the same county, about 1840', N.S., 30, 1914, p.205-7. Medieval - 19th c.

GERNON

ROUND, J. Horace. 'Notes on the pedigree of Gernon', N.S., 3, 1886, p.29-31. Suffolk; medieval.

See also Gresley

GIFFARD

WROTTESLEY, George. 'Dugdale's pedigree of Giffard of Brimsfield', N.S., 16, 1900, p.24-6. Brimpsfield, Gloucestershire; 12-13th c.

GIFFORD

HARWOOD, H. W. Forsyth. 'The extinct baronetcy of Gifford of Burstall', N.S., 35, 1919, p.7-16 & 88-92. London & Burstall, Leicestershire; 16-18th c. Includes monumental inscriptions and parish register extracts, with wills.

GILL

DANIEL, W. E. 'A page of clerical history', 5, 1881, p.81-7. Nathaniel Gill, rector of Burgh, Norfolk, 17th c.

GILLMAN

GILLMAN, Herbert Webb. 'The Gillman family and some myths', N.S., 14, 1898, p.152-62. 16-19th c.

RYE, Walter. 'The Gillman or Gilman family', N.S., 13, 1897, p.16-19. Review article.

GLEDSTANE

GLADSTONE, Francis M. 'The Gledstanes of Gledstanes and Coklaw, 1296-1741', N.S., 9, 1893, p.153-7. Gledstanes, Lanarkshire, & Coklaw, Roxburghshire; includes pedigree, 13-18th c.

GLYNN

BEAZLEY, F. C. 'The pedigree of Glynn of Glynn, in the county of Cornwall, and of Liverpool, in the County Palatine of Lancaster', N.S., 24, 1908, p.145-63. 15-19th c., includes wills.

BEAZLEY. F. C. 'Additions to the pedigree of Glynn', N.S., 33, 1917, p.238-40. Devon and Lancashire; 18-19th c.

BEAZLEY, F. C. 'Further notes on the family of Glynn', N.S., 25, 1909, p.266. Extracts from Cardinham, Cornwall, bishops' transcripts; 17th c.

GODFREY

See Hanckwitz

GODIN

CARMICHAEL, Evelyn G. M. 'Family note book of Stephen Peter Godin', N.S., 28, 1912, p.129-41. London; 18th c.

GOET

ROUND, J. H. 'Pedigree of Goet', N.S., 4, 1887, p.159. Essex; 12-13th c.

GOLIGHTLY

See Portales

GOODDAY

'Memoranda relating to the family of Goodday, Co. Middlesex and Suffolk', 3, 1879, p.51-3. Extracts from parish registers, etc., 17-18th c.

GOODRIDGE

See Lisle-Taylor

GOULDSMYTH

See Minshull

GRAHAM

See Portales

GRANT

GRANT, A. R. 'The chiefs of Grant', N.S., 1, 1884, p.214-24. Scotland; Grant family.

GREEN

'An account of the family of Green of Dunsby, Co. Lincoln', 1, 1887, p.55-63. 17-19th c., includes list of family portraits.

'Additions to Green pedigree', 1, 1877, p.395. 18-19th c.

GREENSTREET

'In memoriam: James Harris Greenstreet', N.S., 8, 1892, p.147.

GREGORY

See Smart

GRESLEY

CARTER, William F. 'Gresley and Gernon', N.S., 35, 1919, p.176-7. Wiltshire; 15th c.

GREVIS

GREEN, Everard. 'Pedigree of the family of Grevis of Moseley Hall, in the parish of Kings Norton, Co. Worcester', 6, 1882, p.304-9.

GREY

SMITH, J. C. C. 'Margaret, widow of Richard Grey, 3rd Earl of Kent', 2, 1877, p.388-9. 16th c.

GRIMSTON

MOOR, C. 'The early Grimstons', N.S., 29, 1913, p.129-44. Yorkshire; 13-15th c.

GROVE

PINK, W. D. 'Barony of Fitzwarine: Grove family', 5, 1881, p.32.

GURDUN

BAIN, Joseph. 'Selborne Priory charters: Sir Adam Gurdun', N.S., 11, 1895, p.10. Hampshire; Gurdun family, 13th c.

BAIN, Joseph. 'Sir Adam Gurdun of Selborne', N.S., 4, 1887, p.1-4. See also p.106-7 & 124. Hampshire; 13-14th c.

GWAETHFOED

WATKIN, T. M. J. 'The two Gwaethfoeds', N.S., 15, 1899, p.17-21. Welsh princes, 10-11th c.

HALLEY

McPIKE, Eugene F. 'Some material for a pedigree of Dr. Edmond Halley', N.S., 25, 1909, p.5-14. See also p.143-4 & 207, & 271-2; 34, 1918, p.116. London; 17th c. Includes wills.

HAMILTON

BAIN, Joseph. 'The Hamilton family and its cadets', N.S., 16, 1900, p.73-5. See also 19, 1903, p.143-4. Scotland, 16-19th c.

HARWOOD, H. W. Forsyth. 'The genealogy of the family of Hamilton of Ypres in Flanders, and afterwards of London', N.S., 14, 1898, p.264-71. 17-18th c.

MURRAY, Keith W. 'An incident in the history of the Hamilton family', N.S., 20, 1804, p.1-6. See also p.144. Scotland; 16-17th c.

See also Fitzgilbert

HAMLYN

See Ashmole

HANBURY

APPLETON, Lewis. 'Seal of Philip de Hanbury, 1363', N.S., 24, 1908, p.242-3.

HANCKWITZ

WAGNER, Henry. 'A tentative pedigree of Hanckwitz, known later as Godfrey', N.S., 26, 1910, p.244-5. See also p.62-3. London; 18th c.

HARENC

WAGNER, Henry. 'The Huguenot refugee family of Harenc', N.S., 32, 1916, p.193-5.

HARINGTON

POYNTON, Francis J. 'Who was Margaret, wife of William, V Lord Harington, 1418?' N.S., 9, 1893, p.78. Includes will of Robert Hylle of Spareton, Somerset.

HARRIS

SMITH, J. Challenor. 'A half-forgotten explorer', N.S., 28, 1912, p.233. Includes pedigree of William Harris, 18-19th c.

HARRISON

'Extracts from the parish register of West Quantoxhead, Co. Somerset, relating to the family of Harrison', 2, 1878, p.24-6. 16-18th c.

HARVARD

RENDLE, W. 'Harvard University, U.S., and the Harvards of Southwark', N.S., 1, 1884, p.107-11. See also p.182-3, & 3, 1886, p.188; Surrey.

HATCH

DRAKE, Sir William R. 'Families of Hatch in Devon', 1, 1877, p.313-20 & 368-75. 13-18th c.

See also Audley

HATLEY

SMITH, W. H. 'A sacrament certificate', N.S., 1, 1884, p.106-7. Certifying the attendance at communion of Griffith Hatley of Maidstone, Kent, 1773.

HAWARDEN

WALSH, V. Hussey. 'The pedigree of the late Henry Hawarden-Gellibrand-Fazakerley and the descent to him of Fazakerley Hall, Gellibrand Hall, and Lower House in Widnes', N.S., 33, 1917, p.178-83 & 223-37. Fazakerley, Chorley, and Widnes, Lancashire; includes pedigrees, 13-20th c., of Fazakerley, Gellibrand & Hawarden.

HAWLEY

S. 'Does an heir to the Barony of Hawley exist?', 1, 1877, p.161-3. Somerset; 17-18th c.

HAYNES

WAGNER, Henry. 'The descendants of Hopton Haynes', N.S., 20, 1904, p.280-81. London; pedigree, 12-18th c.

HENSLOWE

RENDLE, William. 'Philip Henslowe', N.S., 4, 1887, p.149-59. Of Southwark, Surrey; 16-17th c.

HERBERT

BIRD, W. H. B. 'Herbert son of Aubri', N.S., 33, 1917, p.145-51. See also p.279. Lincolnshire; 11-12th c.

HERON

See Smart

HILL

COKAYNE, G. E. 'Pedigree of the family of Hill, of Rothwell, Co. Northampton', N.S., 15, 1899, p.103-12, 178-85 & 228-40. 17-19th c., includes wills, monumental inscriptions and parish register extracts.

HOLLAND

RYLANDS, J. Paul. 'A pedigree of the family of Holland of Mobberley, in the county of Chester, drawn about the year 1650', N.S., 31, 1915, p.93-5. 15-17th c.

See also Dukinfield

HONYWOOD

ELLIS, William Smith. 'The pedigree of Honywood of Horsham', N.S., 4, 1887, p.22-4. Sussex; 16-17th c.

HOOPER

H., R. P. 'Extracts from the registers of Salisbury Cathedral relating to the family of Hooper, of New Sarum and Boveridge', N.S., 2, 1885, p.42. Wiltshire; 16-17th c.

HORDE

See Roberts

HOUSTON

S., S. 'Houston of that Ilk', 5, 1881, p.22-3. Renfrewshire.

HOWARD

ELLIS, W. S. 'Howard family', 2, 1878, p.349-53. 17-18th c.

ELLIS, W. S. 'Sir Charles Howard of Merrow, Knight', 5, 1881, p.106-9. Surrey; 17th c.

RYE, Walter. 'Doubtful Norfolk pedigrees, no. 1: Howard', 2, 1878, p.337-43. Medieval.

HUCHYNS

See Tyndale

HUNNINGS

FOSTER, W. E. Some notes on the families of Hunnings of South Lincolnshire, London and Suffolk. Exeter: W. Pollard & Co., 1912. Supplement to Genealogist, N.S., 28-29.

See also Newcomen

HUNTER

S. 'Notice of a recent case in the Court of Session, Scotland, as to the surname and arms of Hunter of Hunterston', 6, 1882, p.310-15. Ayrshire.

HURST

LOWE, A. E. Lawson. 'The family of Hurst of Hurst, in the parish of Ashton-under-Lyne, Co. Lancaster', 5, 1881, p.139-41.

HYLLE

See Harington

INGOLDSBY

'Pedigree of Ingoldsby', N.S., 3, 1886, p.136-9. Buckinghamshire; 16-18th c.

IRELAND

RYLANDS, J. Paul. 'Pedigree of Ireland, of the Hutt, in Halewood, Co. Lancaster', N.S., 34, 1918, p.6-8. Medieval - 17th c.

ISAAC

'Pedigree of Isaac of Westdown, etc., Co. Devon', 4, 1880, p.118-21. 16-18th c., includes pedigree of Codrington, 14-17th c., and extracts from Atherington parish register.

ISHAM

RYE, Walter. 'Isham family memoranda', 2, 1878, p.241-50, & 3, 1879, p.274-80. See also p.300. Northamptonshire; 16-17th c.

JACKSON

CLAY, C. T. 'The family of Jackson of Wooldale in the county of York', N.S., 37, 1921, p.29-33.

JOHNSON

GREEN, Everard. 'Pedigree of Johnson of Ayscough-fee Hall, Spalding, Co. Lincoln', 1, 1877, p.105-15. 16-19th c.

JOINVILLE

See Lacy

JULLIAN

WAGNER, Henry. 'Pedigree of Jullian', 6, 1882, p.47. London; 18-19th c.

KEKEWICH

CARTER, W. F. 'The Kekewich family', N.S., 26, 1910, p.8-15 & 72-82. 15-16th c., includes extracts from early Chancery proceedings .

CARTER, William Fowler. 'The name and family of Kekewich', 6, 1882, p.8-11. Cornwall; 14-15th c.

KENRICK

CARTER, W. F. 'Notes on Kenrick families', N.S., 1908, p.15-22, 96-103, 164-72 & 244-9; 25, 1909, p.15-21, 120-5, 175-81 & 215-23; 29, 1913, p.272, & 36, 1920, p.56. 14-20th c., includes a few wills.

KENT

'A pedigree of the family of Kent, and their descendants', 2, 1878, p.185-92. London & Middlesex; 18-19th c.

See also Grey

KER

KETT, Marion. 'Some particular Sasines concerning the family of the Kers of Kersland and Trearne', N.S., 36, 1920, p.70-74. Ayrshire; 17th c. sasines.

KERR

C. 'Family of Kerr and Carr', 3, 1879, p.88-90. Lincolnshire; 15-17th c.

S. 'Content for precedency between the Kerr families of Cessford and Fernihurst', 2, 1878, p.380-3. Roxburghshire; 17th c.

S. 'Kerr of Ancrum, Earl of Ancrum and Marquis of Lothian', 2, 1878, p.289-94. Scotland; 16-17th c.

S. 'Kerr of Fernihurst, Baron Jedburgh', 2, 1878, p.282-9. Roxburghshire; 16-17th c.

'Kerr of Gateshaw', 3, 1879, p.246-50. Roxburghshire; 15-18th c.

'Sir Thomas Kerr, of Redden, and his descendants: a neglected genealogy', 2, 1878, p.137-42 & 176-80. Roxburghshire; 17-19th c.

KILLINGTREE

See Duppa

KINGSLEY

PINK, W. D. 'Kingsley of Sarratt, Canterbury, and London', N.S., 29, 1913, p.212-24, & 30, 1914, p.35-8 & 86-94. Sarratt, Hertfordshire, & Canterbury, Kent; 16-19th c., includes wills.

KINGSMILL

ABBOTT, Thomas Kingsmill. 'Royal descent of Kingsmill', N.S., 12, 1896, p.76-8. Medieval - 16th c.

KINLOCH

WAGNER, Henry. 'Descendants of Sir James Kinloch, Bart.', N.S., 14, 1898, p.200-203, & 261-3., N.S., 15, 1899, p.49-51. Holland; includes pedigrees of De Coppet and De Rham, 18-19th c.

KNOLLYS

PEARMAN, M. T. 'The Banbury peerage', N.S., 1, 1884, p.42-5. Knollys family; 17th c.

PEARMAN, M. T. 'Sir Francis Knollys', N.S., 1, 1884, p.139-44.

KNOWLES

C[OKAYNE], G. E. 'Pedigree of Knowles of London', N.S., 18, 1902, p.225-30. 17th c., includes extracts from parish registers, and wills.

LACAUX

WAGNER, Henry. 'Pedigree of the Huguenot refugee family of Lacaux', N.S., 25, 1909, p.246-7. London; 18th c.

LACY

WATSON, G. W. 'The families of Lacy, Geneva, Joinville, and La Marche', N.S., 21, 1905, p.1-16, 73-82, 163-72 & 234-43. 12-14th c.

LA MARCHE

See Lacy

LAMBE

GUIMARAENS, A. J. C. 'Notes on the family of Lambe of Co. Durham', N.S., 25, 1910, p.143-6. 18th c.

LA PRIMAUDAYE

WAGNER, Henry. 'The Huguenot refugee family of La Primaudaye', N.S., 23, 1907, p.171-3. London; 18-19th c.

LATHAM

See Mascy

LAWFORD

AMES, Reginald. 'Pedigrees of the family of Lawford', N.S., 8, 1892, p.184(f). Various counties; 17-19th c.

See also Maudit

LEE

LEA, J. Henry. 'Genealogical notes on the family of Lee of Quarrendon', N.S., 8, 1892, p.226-32; 9, 1893, p.18-26, 157-61 & 227-31; 10, 1894, p.71-8 & 229-37; 11, 1895, p.20-8; 12, 1896, p.186-92; 13, 1897, p.120-6 & 229-36; 14, 1898, p.127-31 & 166-70. See also 11, 1895, p.63-4. Not continued. Berkshire; includes parish register extracts, monumental inscriptions, wills, inquisitions post mortem, etc., relating to Lee and many associated families, 16-18th c.

LEA, J. Henry. 'Lee of Pocklington', N.S., 11, 1895, p.203-11. Yorkshire; includes pedigree, 17-18th c., with wills and parish register abstracts.

LEE, Frederick George. 'Lee pedigree', 1, 1877, p.177-80. Cheshire; medieval - 17th c.

SUCKLING, F. H. 'Some notes on the Lee family of Lawshall, in the county of Suffolk', N.S, 23, 1907, p.137-43. See also p.271-2. 17-18th c.

LE FAUCONER

'Le Fauconer and Falkener pedigree', N.S, 1, 1884, p.241-2. Rutland; includes extracts from parish register, 16-18th c., with pedigree.

'Pedigree of the family of Le Fauconer, Falkener, and Fawkener in Leicestershire and Rutland', N.S., 1, 1884, p.129-39. 11-19th c.

LEMAN

LEEMAN, W. J. 'The Leman baronetcy', N.S., 21, 1905, p.227-33. Suffolk; 17-19th c.

LE POHER

ROUND, J. H. 'Le Poher family', N.S., 12, 1896, p.215-6. See also p.221-3 & 13, 1897, p.15-16 & 131-2. 12-13th c.

'Roger, Bishop of Salisbury', N.S., 10, 1894, p.207. 12th c., Le Poher family?

LESLY

BAIN, Joseph. 'John Lesly, Bishop of Ross (a vindication)', N.S., 16, 1900, p.26-7. See also p.219-22, & 17, 1901, p.5-6 & 158-61.

LETTIN

LATTING, John J. 'Pedigree of Lettin', N.S., 5, 1888, p.20-21. 17th c. Dutch immigrants.

LEVESON

'Leveson family: register extracts from Trentham, Staffordshire', 2, 1878, p.84-7. 16-17th c. Also includes some from Lilleshull, Shropshire.

LEVETT

SANBORN, V. C. 'Thomas Levet and Richard Berry', N.S., 31, 1915, p.79-93. Yorkshire; 17th c. Includes wills of Thomas Levett of High Melton, Yorkshire, 1622, Roger Dale of Tekesore, Rutland, 1622; Richard Berry, 1651.

LINCOLN

KIRK, R. E. G. 'The family of Lincoln', N.S., 6, 1890, p.129-39. See also 7, 1891, p.62 & 178-9; 8, 1892, p.1-6, 81-91, 148-9; 9, 1893. Lincolnshire; Debate with J. H. Round; includes 12-14th c. pedigree.

See also Adeliza

LINDSAY

SITWELL, Sir George. 'The origin of the Lindsays', N.S, 12, 1896, p.1-6. See also p.75 & 152-3; N.S., 13, 1897, p.19-20.

LINGEN

BRADNEY, Joseph Alfred. 'Pedigree of Lingen of Sutton, Herefordshire', 5, 1881, p.137-8. 17-19th c.

LIRON

WAGNER, Henry. 'Pedigree of Liron', N.S., 21, 1905, p.50-51. London; 18-19th c.

LISLE

MARILLIER, Henry. 'The descendants of Alice Lisle', 6, 1882, p.12-15. Includes pedigree, 17-19th c., Lisle, Whitaker and Maudslay families.

STEPHENSON, C. A. 'Descendants of Alice Lisle, beheaded 1685', 5, 1881, p.186. 17-18th c.

LISLE-TAYLOR

PULMAN, J., & WADE, Edward Fry. 'Pedigree of Lisle-Taylor and Goodridge', 7, 1883, p.267-9. Hampshire; 16-19th c.

LOMBARD

WAGNER, Henry. 'Peter Lombard of Nismes and his immediate descendants', N.S., 35, 1919, p.52-5. 17-19th c. Includes Walpole family of Norfolk.

LOVEL

BAIN, Joseph. 'The Lovels of Castle Cary and Hawick', N.S., 4, 1887, p.214-5. Somerset & Roxburghshire; 13-14th c.

LUCADON

Wagner, Henry. 'Fragmentary pedigree of the Huguenot refugee family of Lucadon', N.S., 27, 1911, p.230-1. See also 28, 1912, p.64. London; 18th c.

LUCY

KIRK, R. E. G. 'The Countess Lucy: singular or plural?' N.S., 5, 1888, p.60-75, 131-44 & 153-73. 11-12th c., daughter of Thorold the Sheriff.

ROUND, J. H. 'The heirs of Richard de Lucy', N.S., 15, 1899, p.129-33. Includes pedigree, 12-13th c.

LUMLEY

BIRD, W. H. B. 'Lumley: some female descents', N.S., 35, 1919, p.1-7. Co. Durham; 13-14th c.

LUSIGNAN

See Mauclerk

LYNNE

GREEN, Everard. 'Pedigree of the family of Lynne of Southwick, Co. Northampton', 1, 1877, p.345-54. See also 2, 1878, p.71-2. 15-18th c.

LYTTELTON

CARTER, William. 'Pedigree of the family of Lyttelton', 37, 1921, p.1-29. Worcestershire; medieval.

GRAZEBROOK, H. Sydney. 'The Lytteltons of Naunton and Studley', 3, 1879, p.97-104. Worcestershire; 17-18th c.

MACDONALD

'Pedigree of MacDonald of Sanda', 5, 1881, p.208-10. Argyll; 19th c.

McGROUTHER

MACGREGOR, John. 'The McGrouthers of Meigor in Glenartney', N.S., 35, 1919, p.65-81. Perthshire; 16-19th c.

MACKAY

CARTER, William Fowler. 'The Mackays of Melness and Torboll, and the Mackays of Bigghouse', 5, 1881, p.20-22. Sutherland; includes pedigree, 18-19th c.

MADDOCKES

HOLDEN, E. Lofft. 'Entries relating to the Maddockes family', 3, 1879, p.141-3. Suffolk & Surrey; 17-18th c; includes will of Kinsman Singleman, 1769.

MAINWARING

See Ashmole

MALECARE DE PRATVIEL

WAGNER, Henry. 'Fragmentary pedigree of Malecare de Pratviel', N.S., 25, 1925, p.196-7. 18th c.

MALLORY

See Duppa

MALPAS

SWETTENHAM, Sir Alexander. 'The Barony of Malpas', N.S., 32, 1916, p.83-4. Cheshire; 11-12th c.

MANDEVILLE

FOWLER, G. Herbert. 'Mandeville, Fitz Geoffrey, and Beauchamp of Eaton', N.S., 29, 1913, p.78-85'. Cheshire; includes pedigree, 12-13th c.

MANN

'Extracts from the parish registers of Little Ouseburn, Co. York, of entries relating to the family of Mann, between the years 1565 and 1694', 7, 1883, p.237-9.

MARKHAM

MARSHALL, G. W. 'Extracts from the register of Ollerton, Co. Nottingham, relating to the family of Markham', N.S., 4, 1887, p.54. 17-18th c.

MARRIOTT-DODINGTON

'Pedigree of Marriott-Dodington of Horsington', 1, 1877, p.81-84. Somerset; 17-19th c.

MARSH

C[OKAYNE], G. E. Some notice of various families of the name of Marsh. Exeter: W. Pollard & Co., 1900. Supplement to Genealogist, N.S., 16-17.

See also Duppa

MARSHALL

M[ARSHALL], G. W. 'The Marshalls of Exeter', 4, 1880, p.11-17. Devon; 17th c.

R., J. P. 'George William Marshall, York Herald', N.S., 22, 1906, p.198-202. Includes list of his printed genealogical works.

'Extracts from the parish registers of Egton, near Whitby, Co. York', 2, 1878, p.18. Relating to the Marshall family, 1628-1771.

'Extracts from the parish registers of Harswell, Co. York', 2, 1878, p.234. Relating to the Marshall family, 18th c.

'Extracts from the parish registers of Holme on Spalding Moor, Co. York', 2, 1878, p.233. Relating to the Marshall family, 18th c.

'Extracts from the parish registers of Whitby, Co. York, from 1600 to 1795', 2, 1878, p.232-33. Relating to the Marshall family, 17-18th c.

'Extracts from the parish registers of Winteringham, Co. York', 2, 1878, p.231-2. Relating to the Marshall family, 16-17th c.

'Marshall', 1, 1877, p.117. 16-17th c., includes extracts from Middleton, Yorkshire, parish register.

'Pedigree of Marshall of Urswick, Hadham, Blewbury, Bosbury, etc', 5, 1881, p.125-30. Urswick, Lancashire; Hadham, Hertfordshire, Blewbury, Berkshire, & Bosbury, Herefordshire; includes pedigree, 16-17th c., and wills of John & William Marshall, 1646 & 1676.

MARSHAM

BANNERMAN, W. Bruce. 'Marsham pedigree', N.S., 17, 1901, p.13. Kent; 17-18th c.

MARTYN

See De Braose

MARWOOD

MUNK, William. 'Marvodia: being an account of the last illness of James I, and of the post-mortem examination of his body, from a ms. long in the possession of the Marwoods of Honiton, to which are appended some notes in illustration of the Marwoods and of their descendants', N.S., 1, 1884, p.228-40; 2, 1885, p.15-29, 123-8 & 255-61. Devon; Includes pedigree of Marwood, 17-19th c., with wills.

MASCY

B., W. H. B. 'Notes on the Mascy and Latham pedigrees', N.S., 16, 1900, p.201-6. Lancashire; includes pedigree, 14th c.

See also Tillesley

MASON

SANBORN, V. C. 'Sir John Mason, and the Masons of Hampshire', N.S., 34, 1918, p.34-40. 16-17th c., includes inquisition post mortem of Anthony Weekes, 1607.

MASSE

WAGNER, Henry. 'Pedigree of the Huguenot family of Masse, N.S., 24, 1908, p.40-41. 17-18th c. London; female descent to Olivier.

MASSERES

See Duprat de Charreau

MASSINGBERD

SYMPSON, E. Marsel. 'The late Rev. W. O. Massingberd', N.S., 27, 1911, p.123.

MATY

WAGNER, Henry. 'The Huguenot refugee family of Maty', N.S., 22, 1906, p.188-9. 18th c.

MAUCLERK

WATSON, G. W. 'The marriages of Pierre Mauclerc, sometime Duke of Brittany and Earl of Richmond, N.S., 36, 1920, p.1-8. 13th c., includes pedigree of the Counts of Eu of the house of Lusignan.

MAUDIT

AMES, Reginald. Descendants of Isaac Maudit, 4, 1880, p.87-9. Pedigree, 18-19th c., shewing descent of Wright & Lawford.

'Pedigree of Maudit', 1, 1877, p.132-7. 16-17th c.

MAUDSLAY

See Lisle

MAUNSELL

COKAYNE, G. E. 'Pedigree of Maunsell, formerly of Chicheley, Bucks., and subsequently, after 1622, of Thorpe Malsor, Co. Northampton, enlarged and continued from that entered in the visitation of Essex, A.D. 1634', N.S., 19, 1903, p.12-18, 88-96, 153-8 & 235-41. Includes wills, monumental inscriptions, & parish register extracts.

MENZIES

STEWART, C. Poyntz. 'The red and white book of Menzies', N.S., 22, 1906, p.94-105. Review article; Scotland.

MERTTINS

See Bennett

METCALFE

See Pointer

METHVEN

'Methven of that Ilk: a doubtful pedigree', 4, 1880, p.59-61. Perthshire.

MEULAN

See Beaumont

MICKLETHWAITE

'Sir John Micklethwait', 1, 1877, p.248. Yorkshire; 17th c.

MILL

See Sandys

MILTON

See Minshull

MINSHULL

SHARPE, T. E. 'Milton, Minshull and Gouldsmyth', 2, 1878, p.309-15. Shropshire families, 16-18th c.

MOORE

WALSH, V. Hussey. 'The Anglo-Norman Moores in Ireland', N.S., 33, 1917, p.1-8. 15-18th c.

WALSH, V. Hussey. 'The Moores of the City of Drogheda', N.S., 33, 1917, p.127-8. 17-18th c.

See also Du Moulin Browne

MORAY

BAIN, Joseph. 'Notes on the De Moravia or Moray family', N.S., 16, 1900, p.137-9. Scotland; 14th c.

'Murrays of Dollerie, near Crieff, Perthshire, oldest cadets of the family of Ochtertyre', 7, 1883, p.15-19. 15-19th c. Name actually spelt Moray.

MORDAUNT

'Mordaunt family', 7, 1883, p.20-21. Extracts from Lowick, Northamptonshire, parish register, 16-18th c.

MORTIMER

WATSON, G. W. 'Geoffrey de Mortemer and his descendants', N.S., 22, 1906, p.1-16. 14-16th c.

MOSELEY

HOLDEN, E. L. 'Moseley family: extracts from the registers of Owsden, Co. Suffolk', 3, 1879, p.53-4. 17-18th c.

MOURIER DE LALANDE

See Gaury

MOUTRAY

MOUTRAY, J. A. 'Notes on the name of Moutray', 7, 1883, p.24-7. Scotland; 13-18th c.

MURRAY

MACGREGOR, John. 'Notes on Murray of Newran or Woodend', N.S., 28, 1912, p.17-23. Perthshire; 16-17th c.

MURRAY, Keith W. 'The outlaw Murray', 12, 1896, p.217-21. Scotland; 14-15th c.

MURRAY, Keith W. 'A short account of the Murrays of Melgum', N.S., 11, 1895, p.1-9. Selkirkshire; includes pedigree, 17-18th c.

PAUL, J. Balfour. 'The Murrays of Romanno, Broughton and Stenhope', N.S., 15, 1899, p.193-202. Broughton, Peebles; 16-18th c.

NEALE

'A Baronet's warrant, 1646: Sir William Neale of Wollaston, Co. Northampton, Kt', 6, 1882, p.211-12

NEVILE

NEVILE, Alice E. 'Pedigree of Nevile of Thorney', N.S., 27, 1911, p.232. Nottinghamshire; includes folded pedigree, 14-20th c.

NEVILL

MASSINGBERD, W. O. 'Lincolnshire Nevill families', N.S., 27, 1911, p.1-7. Includes pedigree, 12-15th c.

MASSINGBERD, W. O. 'Nevill of Habrugh, Bigby and Hale', N.S., 25, 1909, p.1-4. See also p.143. Lincolnshire; 12-13th c. Includes deeds.

MASSINGBERD, W. O. 'Nevill of Laceby, Sturton and Appleby, Co. Lincoln', N.S., 21, 1905, p.217-21. 13-14th c., includes pedigree.

NEVILL, Edmund R. 'Nevill of Combe Nevill (Surrey and Essex)', N.S., 32, 1916, p.160-63. 13-16th c.

NEVILL, Edmund R. 'Nevill of Essex', N.S., 27, 1911, p.116-7. 14-15th c.

NEVILL, Edmund R. 'Nevill of Essex', N.S., 35, 1919, p.81-7. Includes pedigree, 16-17th c.

NEVILL, Edmund R. 'Nevill of Faldingworth and Snitterby', N.S., 28, 1912, p.209-15. See also 29, 1913, p.64. Lincolnshire; 12-14th c.

NEVILL, Edmund R. 'Nevill of Herts', N.S., 26, 1910, p.24-6. Includes pedigree, 12-14th c.

NEVILL, E. R. 'Nevill of Rolleston, Grove and Thorney', N.S., 33, 1917, p.154-6. Rolleston, Leicestershire; Grove & Thorney, Nottinghamshire.

NEVILL, Edmund R. 'Nevill of Thornton Bridge and Cundall', N.S., 33, 1917, p.9-15. Yorkshire; includes pedigree, 13-16th c.

NEVILL, Edmund. 'The Nevills of Essex: a genealogical puzzle', N.S., 23, 1907, p.143-5. See also p.270-71 & 24, 1908, p.69-71 & 143-4. Includes pedigree, 12-14th c.

NEVILL, Edmund R. 'The Nevills of Suffolk', N.S., 31, 1915, p.141-53. 15-19th c.

NEVILL, E. R. 'Thorold de Nevill', N.S., 34, 1918, p.117-9. Yorkshire; 12-14th c.

See also Tailbois

NEWCOMEN

FOSTER, W. E. 'Pedigree of the families of Newcomen and Hunnings, of Co. Lincoln', N.S., 19, 1903, p.164-9. 16-19th c.

NEWPORT

'Newport of Hanley Court, Co. Worcester', 1, 1877, p.202-5 & 213-7. See also 2, 1878, p.250 & 3, 1879, p.144. 16-18th c.

NICHOLETTS

MARSHALL, George W. 'Pedigree of Nicholetts of the Hill in the parish of Eastham, Co. Worcester, and of Hopton Sollers, Co. Hereford', 1, 1877, p.233-8. See also 2, 1878, p.250. Medieval - 17th c.

NOBLE

BLAYDES, F. A. 'Noble family', N.S., 1, 1884, p.91-2. 17th c. notes from a family bible.

NORMANVILLE

SITWELL, Sir George R. 'Gerard de Normanville', N.S., 13, 1897, p.11-15. Yorkshire & Lincolnshire; 12-13th c.

NORTHCLIFFE

NORCLIFFE, C. B. 'Sir Thomas Northcliffe: diploma Perthense honorabilis Fairfacis Norcleiff chiliarchae legali, 1712', 1, 1877, p.240-41. Yorkshire; conferment of the freedom of the city of Perth.

ODARD

ROUND, J. H. 'Odard of Carlisle', N.S., 8, 1892, p.200-4. Cumberland.

ROUND, J. H. 'Odard the sheriff', N.S., 5, 1888, p.25-8. See also 9, 1893, p.59. Northumberland; 12th c.

OFFLEY

BOWER, G. C. 'A manuscript relating to the family of Offley', N.S., 19, 1903, p.1-11, 83-8 & 149-53. Staffordshire and London; 16th c.

BOWER G. C., & HARWOOD, H.W.F. 'Pedigree of Offley', N.S., 19, 1903, p.217-31; 20, 1904, p.49-56, 78-86, 197-9 & 268-74. London, Staffordshire & Cheshire, 16-19th c.

OGILVIE

MURRAY, Keith W. 'The outfit of a naval cadet in the reign of George II', N.S., 25, 1909, p.264-6. Bill for Alexander Ogilvie.

OGILVY

RAMSAY, Sir James Henry. 'Ogilvy of Auchterhouse, Ogilvys of Airlie, Ogilvys of Inverquharity, and Ogilvys of Clova, N.S., 35, 1919, p.162-75. Forfar; 14-17th c.

OGLE

GREEN, Everard. 'Notes to the pedigree of Ogle of Pinchbeck', 1, 1877, p.321. See also 2, 1878, p.28. Lincolnshire.

GREEN, Everard. 'Pedigree of Ogle of Pinchbeck, Co. Lincoln', 1, 1877, p.270 (f). 16-17th c.

OLDFIELD

'Pedigree of the family of Oldfield of Spalding, Co. Lincoln', 1, 1877, p.242-7. See also p.278 & 5, 1881, p.123-4. 17-18th c.

ORBY

GREEN, Everard. 'Pedigree of the family of Orby of Croyland Abbey, Co. Lincoln', 3, 1879, p.271-3.

ORMONDE

HALL, Hubert. 'The Ormonde attainders', N.S., 1, 1884, p.76-80; 2, 1885, p.186-9.

See also Butler

OSBERT

BIRD, W. H. B. 'Osbert the sheriff', N.S., 32, 1916, p.1-6, 73-83, 153-60 & 227-32. Lincolnshire, 12th c., descent through Chamberlain, 13th c.

OSBORNE

COKAYNE, G. E. 'Pedigrees of the families of Osborne and Buckby', N.S., 24, 1908, p.1-14. London & Bedfordshire; 16-18th c.

OVERBURY

MARSHALL, G. W. 'The Overbury family', 1, 1877, p.267-70. See also 2, 1878, p.364-5. Includes will of Sir Nicholas Overbury of Bourton on the Hill, Gloucestershire, 1640, with extracts from London parish registers, 16-17th c. Continuation of notes previously published in the Herald & genealogist.

'Pedigree of Overbury', 1, 1877, p.271-6. Gloucestershire & Warwickshire; 16-17th c.

PARADISE

KITE, Edward and SCHOMBERG, Arthur. 'Family of Paradise', N.S., 37, 1921, p.74-84 & 151-4. Wiltshire; 16-18th c. Includes wills.

PAYNE

See Boyville

PELHAM

E., W. S. 'Pelham: a doubtful peerage pedigree', 4, 1880, p.213-25. See also 5, 1881, p.105-6. Sussex; 13-14th c.

PERCY

WATSON, G. W. 'Philippe de Strabolgy: a fourteenth century abduction', N.S., 29, 1913, p.1-11. Wife of Ralph de Percy.

PERRONET

WAGNER, Henry. 'Pedigree of Perronet and Thompson', N.S., 13, 1897, p.41-5. France; 17-19th c.

PERRYN

See Gerard

PESHALL

FLETCHER, W. G. D. 'The Baronetcy of Peshall', N.S., 28, 1912, p.193-8. Staffordshire; 17th c. Includes wills.

PEYTON

RYE, Walter. 'Peyton family', N.S., 3, 1886, p.28. Kent; certificate of pedigree, 1680.

PHILLIMORE

FLETCHER, W. G. D. 'In memoriam: William Phillimore Watts Phillimore', N.S., 30, 1914, p.107-9.

PIGOT

FALKINGHAM, Chas. C. 'Pigot of Melmorby in Coverdale, and of Clotherham near Ripon, Co. York', 2, 1878, p.294-8.

PLANTAGENET

WATSON, G. W. 'The ascendants of Geoffrey Plantagenet', N.S., 13, 1897, p.1-10. Medieval.

PLAYTER

WADLEY, Thomas P. 'Notes on the family of Playter, or Playters, of Co. Suffolk', N.S., 1, 1884, p.45-9, 169-78 & 243-56. Extracts from parish registers, with many wills.

POINTER

CRUMP, J. Hamerton. 'Pointer pedigree, &c', N.S., 3, 1886, p.101-7 & 232-40. Oxfordshire; 17-18th c., also includes notes on Willoughby, Metcalfe, Williams, & Badgers.

POPE

See Turner

PORT

ROUND, J. H. 'The Ports of Basing', N.S., 18, 1902, p.137-9. Hampshire; 12-13th c.

See also St. John

PORTALES

WAGNER, Henry. 'The Huguenot family of Portales', N.S., 22, 1906, p.50-51. London; 17-19th c. Female descents through Wynantz, Dodd, Golightly, & Graham.

PORTLAND

See Bentinck

POWELL

WOOD, H. J. T. 'A Breconshire pedigree: the families of Powell and Williams, lords of the manor of Llangastey Talyllyn', N.S., 14, 1898, p.141-52. Medieval.

POWIS

HALL, Hubert. 'Some notes on the Powis peerage case in the reign of Elizabeth', N.S., 4, 1887, p.47-9.

POYNTON

HARWOOD, H. W. Forsyth. 'In memoriam', N.S, 33, 1917, p.69-70. [Edward Morris Poynton]

POYNTON, Francis J. 'Poynton and Wyttlebury pedigree', N.S., 10, 1894, p.34-7. Warwickshire; 14-15th c.

'In memoriam: [Francis John Poynton], N.S., 20, 1904, p.210.

PRICHARD

See Smart

PRIME

MARILLIER, Henry. 'Prime of Huntingdon', 6, 1882, p.138-9. 18th c.

PYPER

KING, Edward. 'Pyper of Launceston and Tresmarrow, Cornwall', 6, 1872, p.57-60 123-6. Includes parish register extracts and monumental inscriptions, 16-18th c.

QUINCEY

BAIN, Joseph. 'Thomas de Quincey and his supposed descent from the Earls of Worcester', N.S., 7, 1891, p.17-21.

RAINSFORD

RAINSFORD, F. V. 'Pedigree of Rainsford', 2, 1878, p.105-14. See also p.270, 3, 1879, p.94, & 35, 1919, p.63. 16-19th c.

RAMSAY

RAMSAY, Sir John Henry. 'Notes on early Ramsay pedigrees, A.D. 1200-1600', N.S., 31, 1915, p.1-22. Scotland.

RASBY

'Pedigree of Rasby', 1, 1877, p.92-6. See also 2, 1878, p.30, 96-9, & 4, 1880, p.108. Yorkshire; 13-17th c.

REMINGTON

PRETYMAN, William. 'The Remingtons of Craven, Yorkshire', N.S., 27, 1911, p.129-49.

RERESBY

'A crossbow licence, 1516', N.S., 10, 1894, p.248-9. For Reresby, of Yorkshire.

RICHARDS

SMITH, G. C. Moore. 'Richards of Kentisbury, Co. Devon', N.S., 27, 1911, p.78-81. See also 33, 1917, p.143-4. 17-18th c.

RIDDELL

BAIN, Joseph. 'The Riddells of that ilk, and the Ridels of Blaye, Cranston-Ridel, and Witering, distinct families', N.S., 6, 1890, p.1-3. Medieval; Blaye, Guienne; Cranston-Ridel, Lothian; Witering, Northamptonshire.

RIMMINGTON

RIMMINGTON, William Henry. 'The family of Rimmington, of Gateforth in the parish of Brayton, near Selby, in the county of York (West Riding)', N.S., 36, 1920, p.92-105.

RINGESDUNE

POYNTON, E. M. 'The pedigree of Ringesdune and the manor of Blaysworth', N.S., 22, 1906, p.145-9. Blaysworth, Huntingdonshire; 13th c.

ROUND, J. H. 'The pedigree of Ringesdune, N.S., 18, 1902, p.216-8. Lincolnshire; 12-13th c.

ROBERTS

GRIGSON, Francis. 'Pedigree of Roberts of Willesden, Co. Middlesex, 5, 1881, p.300-307. 16-17th c.

POWELL, Edgar. 'Roberts and Horde families', N.S., 2, 1885, p.46-7. Roberts of Willesden, Middlesex, and Horde of Ewell, Surrey; includes pedigree, 16th c.

ROBINSON

LOWE, A. E. Lawson. 'Pedigree of Robinson', 3, 1879, p.259. Staffordshire & Derbyshire; 17-19th c.

ROBSART

BAIN, Joseph. 'Canon Sir Theodore de Robertsart, knight, a leader of free companions in the fourteenth century', 6, 1890, p.206-7. 14th c.

ROCHESTER

RENSHAW, Walter C. 'The Rochesters of Selmeston, and Jevington, Co. Sussex', N.S., 22, 1906, p.209-11. 17-18th c.

RODNEY

BIRD, W. H. B. 'The origin of the Rodneys', N.S., 26, 1910, p.93-101.

RODNEY, Sir Edward. 'The genealogy of the family of Rodney of Rodney Stoke, as compiled in the seventeenth century by Sir Edward Rodney', N.S., 16, 1900, p.207-14; 17, 1901, p.6-12 & 100-106.

ROLT

ROUND, J. H. 'Sir Thomas Rolt, "President of India"', N.S., 17, 1901, p.145-9. Hertfordshire; 17th c.

ROOKE

ROOKE, H. W. 'Descendants of Giles Rooke, of Romsey and Houghton, Co. Hants', N.S., 37, 1921, p.132-46. 17-19th c.

WAGNER, Henry. 'Pedigree of Rooke, of Co's Kent and Gloucester', 4, 1880, p.195-208. 16-19th c., includes wills, extracts from parish registers, and monumental inscriptions.

ROPER

C[OKAYNE], G. E. 'Family of Roper of Kent, 1581-1660, N.S., 13, 1897, p.140-44.

ROSSE

DENARIUS. 'Rosse of Shepton Beauchamp, Co. Somerset', N.S., 17, 1901, p.72. Pedigree, 18th c.

ROUS

GREEN, Everard. 'Monumental inscriptions to the family of Rous in Wangford church, Co.. Suffolk', N.S., 19, 1903, p.97-100.

RUDKIN

'The Rudkins of the County Carlow', N.S., 21, 1905, p.145-62. See also N.S., 22, 1906, p.208. Includes pedigree, 18-19th c.

RUSSELL

'An Elizabethan christening', N.S., 3, 1886, p.25-7. Of Elizabeth Russell, 1575.

RYE

RYE, Walter. 'The family of Rye, of North Walsham, Norfolk', 1, 1877, p.67-80 & 122-6. 16-19th c.

RYLANDS

RYLANDS, J. Paul. 'Rylands, of the Rylands, within Westhoughton, Co. Lancaster', 4, 1880, p.170-8.

ST. JOHN

ROUND, J. H. 'The families of St. John and of Port', N.S., 16, 1900, p.1-3. 12th c.

ST. LAWRENCE

ROUND, J. H. 'Note on the Essex visitation of 1634 (ed. Harl. Soc.)' N.S., 1, 1884, p.149-50. On entry for the St. Lawrence family.

SAMBORNE

SANBORN, V. C. 'The Samborne ancestry', N.S., 13, 1897, p.145-52. See also 14, 1898, p.72, & 15, 1899, p.264. Wiltshire; medieval.

'Pedigree of Samborne, from visitation of London, 1687', 1, 1877, p.218-9. Somerset and London; 16-18th c.

SANDERSON

BEAZLEY, F. C. 'The diary and pedigree of Christopher Sanderson of Eggleston', N.S., 22, 1906, p.17-25, & 73-82. Co. Durham; 17th c. Includes wills.

SANDYS

SUCKLING, F. H. 'Genealogy in a "Breeches" bible (family of Sandys)", N.S., 31, 1915, p.213-22. Hampshire; 14-17th c., includes will of Sir John Mill, 1646.

SARGENT

WAGNER, Henry. 'Pedigree of Sargent, afterwards Arnold, and Sargent', N.S., 33, 1917, p.189-97. Kent; 18-20th c.

SAVAGE

BELLEWES, G. O. 'Savage of Bobbing Court, Kent', N.S., 29, 1913, p.201-8. 13-15th c.

SAVARY

See De Varenne

SCHOMBERG

'The Dukes of Schomberg', N.S., 33, 1917, p.217-20. See also 34, 1918, p.115-6 & 177-8. Includes will of Charles, Duke of Schomberg, 1693, with 17-18th c. pedigree, etc.

SCOTT

BAIN, Joseph. 'Eskdale and the Scotts of Buccleuch', N.S., 8, 1892, p.94-5. Dumfriesshire & Stirlingshire.

SCRASE

RENSHAW, Walter C. 'Notes on the Scrase family of Co. Sussex', N.S., 20, 1904, p.217-21. 15-18th c.

SELBY

WALFORD, E. 'The late Mr. Walford D. Selby', N.S., 6, 1890, p.65-8.

SELLON

See Boissier

SEYMOUR

See William

SHANK

S. 'Shank of Castlerig', 1, 1877, p.85-92. Scotland; 15-19th c.

SHAPWYK

ROUND, J. Horace. 'The earliest pedigree', N.S., 1887, p.65-8. On the origins of the word 'pedigree', with pedigree of Shapwyk, 14-15th c.

SHENSTONE

G., H. S. 'Shenstone and Spencer families', 2, 1878, p.210-13. Shropshire and Staffordshire; 18-19th c.

SHEPPERDSON

See Stanhope

SHIPMAN

MARSHALL, George W. 'Pedigree of Shipman', N.S., 3, 1886, p.156-63. See also p.255. Nottinghamshire & various other counties; includes wills, 16-17th c.

SILVESTER

WAGNER, Henry. 'Pedigree of the Huguenot refugee family of Silvester', N.S., 20, 1904, p.170-1. 18-19th c.

SIMOND

WAGNER, Henry. 'The Huguenot refugee family of Simond', N.S., 24, 1908, p.193. 18th c.

SINGLEMAN

See Maddockes

SMART

C. 'Notes on the Smart pedigree', 7, 1883, p.22. Northumberland; 17-18th c.

SMART, T. Gregory. 'Descent of Smart of Trewhitt, Co. Northumberland, from Heron, Carr and Alder', N.S., 7, 1891, p.180-91. 14-19th c.

THOMAS, Walter B. 'Descent of Smart of Trewhitt, Co. Northumberland, from Heron, Carr, and Alder', N.S., 6, 1890, p.87-91. 13-18th c.

'Descent of Smart of Trewhitt, Northumberland', N.S., 8, 1892, p.57-60. 15-18th c.

'Descent of Smart, of Trewhitt, Northumberland, from Prichard and Gregory', N.S., 8, 1892, p.111-9. Northumberland, Monmouthshire, and South Wales; 6-19th c.

SMITH

RYLANDS, J. Paul. 'An illuminated pedigree of the family of William Smith, Rouge Dragon Pursuivant of Arms, A.D. 1605', 6, 1882, p.212-6. Cheshire; 15-16th c.

SOMERSET

See William

SOMERVILLE

BAIN, Joseph. 'The dormant Barony of Somerville', N.S., 9, 1893, p.1-4. Scotland; 15-17th c.

BAIN, Joseph. 'The dormant barony of Somerville: a claim disposed of', N.S., 15, 1899, p.65-7. Renfrewshire; 16-17th c.

CAMPBELL, George William. 'The family of Somerville, and the poet of the chase', N.S., 13, 1897, p.73-81 & 152-7. Scotland; includes pedigree, 17-19th c.

SPENCER

See Shenstone

STAFFORD

PINK, W. D. 'Stafford of Southwick, Grafton and Blatherwick', N.S., 31, 1915, p.173-8. Southwick, Wiltshire; Grafton, Worcestershire, and Blatherwick, Northamptonshire; 14-15th c.

See also Ashmole

STANHOPE

GILDERSOME-DICKINSON, G. E. 'Dugdeles visitation of Yorkshire, with additions: Stanhope of Hampull', N.S., 13, 1897, p.208. Includes will of Elizabeth Shepperdson of Owthorpe, Nottinghamshire, 1681.

STANLEY

GREENSTREET, James. 'A hitherto unknown noble writer of Elizabethan comedies', N.S., 7, 1891, p.205-7. Stanley, Earl of Derby .

GREENSTREET, James. 'Further notices of William Stanley, 6th Earl of Derby, K.G., as a poet and dramatist', N.S., 8, 1892, p.8-15.

STAPLEY

HARWOOD, H. W. Forsyth. 'The Baronetcy of Stapley', N.S., 18, 1902, p.140-62. Sussex; 17-18th c., includes Stapley wills, monumental inscriptions, extracts from parish registers, etc.

STEWART

BAIN, Joseph. 'Sir William Stewart of Jedworth, knight, ancestor of the Earl of Galloway', N.S., 2, 1885, p.81-4. Roxburghshire

M., K. W. 'The mother of Jonet Stewart, Lady Fleming', N.S., 8, 1892, p.185-6. Scotland; 16th c.

ROUND, J. H. 'The origin of the Stewarts and their Chesney connexion', N.S., 18, 1902, p.1-16. Medieval.

'Stewarts of Ely', N.S., 8, 1892, p.56-7. Cambridgeshire.

See also Cromwell

STODART

BURNETT, George. 'In memoriam: R. R. Stodart', N.S., 3, 1886, p.129-35.

STRABOLGI

See Percy

STUART

See Cromwell

STUBBS

BELLEWES, G. O. 'Stubbs of Stamford and Nassington', N.S., 25, 1909, p.157-9. Lincolnshire & Northamptonshire.

SULYARD

SCOTT-MURRAY, C. R. 'Pedigree of the family of Sulyard of Wetherden and Haughley, Co. Suffolk, and of Flemings, Co. Essex', 4, 1880, p.226-34. 15-18th c.

SWINTON

SWINTON, George S. C. 'The family of Swinton', N.S., 15, 1899, p.133-40. See also p.205-9, & 16, 1900, p.14-16. Berwickshire & Northumberland.

SWYNNERTON

SWYNNERTON, Charles. 'Notes on the family of Swynnerton', N.S., 31,, 1915, p.69-78. Staffordshire; 14-15th c.

TAILBOIS

FITZ HERBERT, Reginald H. C. 'Original pedigree of Tailbois and Nevill', N.S., 3, 1886, p.31-5 & 107-11. Medieval.

TAILLEFER

BORLASE, William Copeland. 'History of the family of Taillefer, alias Borlase, of Borlas Frank Taillefer in the county of Cornwall', N.S., 2, 1885, p.1-14, 129-41, 225-39 & 283-92; 3, 1886, p.53-63; 4, 1887, p.160-65; 5, 1888, p.29-35. See also 3, 1886, p.125. With folded pedigree. 12-19th c.

TALBOYS

See Blount

TATESHALE

B., W. H. B. 'The Kirkstead chartulary: De Tateshale', N.S., 18, 1902, p.89-92. Lincolnshire; Tateshale family, 11-13th c.

TATTERSHALL

See Fox

TAYLOR

See Lisle-Taylor

THOMPSON

See Perronet

THOROLD

See Lucy

THYNNE

ROUND, J. H. 'The origin of the Thynnes', N.S., 11, 1895, p.193-5. Wiltshire; includes 15-16th c. pedigree.

TILLESLEY

GATFIELD, George. 'A fifteenth century marriage contract', N.S., 7, 1891, p.245-6. Cheshire; marriage of John Tillesley & Jane Mascy.

TIMINS

See Anderson

TINDALE

PRETYMAN, William. 'Family of Tindale', N.S., 26, 1910, p.16-24 & 82-93. Northamptonshire & Norfolk; medieval - 17th c.

TOLLER

GREEN, Everard. 'Toller of Billingborough, Co. Lincoln', 1, 1877, p.184-91. See also p.322-3. 16-19th c. pedigree.

TOUCHET

'A vellum pedigree-roll of the family of Touchet, of Nether Whitley and Buglawton, Co. Chester, and Touchet, Baron Audley of Heleigh, Co. Stafford', N.S., 36, 1920, p.9-21. Medieval.

TOWNSHEND

RYE, Walter. 'Doubtful Norfolk pedigrees, no. II: Townshend', 3, 1879, p.78-9. 14th c.

TRAFFORD

GREEN, Everard. 'Pedigree of Trafford, of Dunton Hall, in the parish of Tydd St. Mary, Co. Lincoln', 2, 1878, p.155-8. 16-18th c.

TRAPAUD

WAGNER, Henry. Pedigree of the Huguenot refugee family of Trapaud, now Adlercron', N.S., 22, 1906, p.258-61. 18-19th c.

TREVIGAR

WAGNER, Henry. 'A Trevigar record', N.S., 30, 1914, p.187-9. London; includes pedigree, 18th c.

TROTTER

ROUND, J. H. 'Trotter "of Byers Hall" ', N.S., 11, 1895, p.129-31. Co. Durham; 14-19th c.

TURNER

NORCLIFFE, Charles Best. 'Pope's maternal ancestry', 4, 1880, 150-3. York; Turner family, 16-17th c.

TWELLS

TOWNSEND, F. 'Pedigree of Twells', 1, 1877, p.35-6. 17th c., from the visitation of Cambridgeshire, 1684.

'Family of Twells', 6, 1881, p.36-46 & 7, 1883, p.163-4. Nottinghamshire, Leicestershire, Warwickshire etc., 17-19th c. Includes parish register extracts, wills, etc.

TYE

SUCKLING, F. H. 'Some notes on the parentage of Dionysia de Tye', N.S., 25, 1909, p.78-82. Norfolk; 14th c.

TYNDALE

GREENFIELD, B. W. 'Notes relating to the family of Tyndale, of Stinchcombe and Nibley in Gloucestershire, the result of an attempt to discover the parentage of William Tyndale alias Huchyns the martyr', 2, 1878, p.1-7, 38-43, 123-8, 159-62, 227-30, 319-26, 356-63 & 369-71. See also p.68. 15-16th c.

GREENFIELD, B. W. 'Pedigree of the family of Tyndale of Stinchcombe and Nibley, Co. Gloucester', 2, 1878, p.373-8. 16-19th c.

UDNY

S. 'Udny of that Ilk', 2, 1878, p.33-7 & 87-90. Aberdeenshire, 15-18th c.

UMFRAMVILLE

WATSON, G. W. 'The Umframvilles, Earls of Angus and Lords of Kyme', N.S., 26, 1910, p.193-211. Scotland; 13-16th c.

URMSTON

PINK, W. D. 'Urmston of Westleigh and Bradshaw of Pennington, Co. Lancaster', N.S., 17, 1901, p.14-16. Pedigrees, 13-17th c.

VAN BORSSELE

WATSON, G. W. 'Wolfart Van Borssele, Earl of Buchan', N.S., 14, 1898, p.10-11. Scotland; 15th c.

VANE

See Fane

VAUGHAN

RYE, Walter. 'Henry Vaughan, the Silurist', 3, 1879, p.33-6. 17th c.

VER

MASSINGBERD, W. O. 'Ver of Bottesford and Goxhill, Co. Lincoln, and Sproatley, Co. York', N.S., 20, 1904, p.73-77. 12th c.

VERDUN

WATSON, G. W. 'John de Verdun', N.S., 25, 1909, p.195. 13th c.

VINCENT

'In memoriam: John A. C. Vincent', N.S., 21, 1905, p.282.

WAKE

ROUND, J. H. 'The pedigree of Wake', N.S., 9, 1893, p.77-8. 12th c.

WALPOLE

GREEN, Everard. 'Walpole of Pinchbeck, Co. Lincoln', 1, 1877, p.6-12. See also p.193 & 2, 1878, p.28. Pedigree, 15-17th c.

RYE, Walter. 'Doubtful Norfolk pedigrees, no. III: Walpole', 3, 1879, p.79-80. See also N.S., 22, 1906, p.207-8. 14th c.

See also Lombard

WALSH

WALSH, V. Hussey. 'The Austrian branches of the family of Walsh', N.S., 17, 1901, p.217-24; 18, 1902, p.79-88.

WALSH, V. Hussey. 'The French branches of the family of Walsh', N.S., 17, 1901, p.36-43, 90-99, & 153-8. 18th c.

WASHINGTON

GREENSTREET, James. 'The ancestry of General Washington', N.S., 7, 1891, p.145-7. Hertfordshire & Essex, 17-18th c.

See also Gale

WEEKES

See Mason

WEGG

ROUND, J. H. 'Pedigree of Wegg', N.S., 11, 1895, p.19. London, 18-19th c.

WHARTON

BAIN, Joseph. 'The Lords Wharton and their shield', N.S., 8, 1892, p.6-7. Westmorland; 14-16th c. See also p.127-9.

WHELER

MARSH, Bower. 'The parentage of Sir William Wheler, knight and baronet', N.S., 25, 1909, p.209-15. London; 16-17th c.

WHELER, Edward G. 'Notes of the life of Sir George Wheler, knight', N.S., 2, 1885, p.202-11. 3; 1886, p.41-9 & 216-20. Middlesex; 18th c. Autobiographical notes.

WHINYATES

WHINYATES, F. T. 'Pedigree of Whinyates of Chellaston, Co. Derby', N.S., 8, 1892, p.52-5. 16-19th c.

WHITAKER

See Lisle

WHITEFOORD

S., S. 'The family of Whitefoord', 4, 1880, p.141-4. See also 5, 1881, p.19-20. Renfrewshire; 18-19th c.

WHITMORE

WHITMORE, William H. 'The Whitmores of Ludson, Co. Salop', N.S., 6, 1890, p.16-19 & 74-8. 16-18th c., includes pedigree.

WHITTINGHAM

'A pedigree of the Cheshire families of Whittingham and Berington, drawn on vellum and painted by the third Randle Holmes of Chester in 1664', N.S., 30, 1914, p.145-9. Cheshire and Lancashire.

WHORWOOD

HARWOOD, H. W. Forsyth, 'Extracts from a note book of John Whorwood, 1619-1626', N.S., 29, 1913, p.50-51. Staffordshire; Whorwood family, 17th c.

WIGAN

ROUND, J. H. 'Wigan the Marshall', N.S., 5, 1888, p.91. 12th c.

WILFORD

MARSHALL, George W. Sir James Wilford, Kt., 4, 1880, p.1-5. 16th c.

WILLESBYE

GREEN, Everard. 'Pedigree of the family of Willesbye of Spalding, Co. Lincoln', 3, 1879, p.138-40. 16-17th c.

WILLIAM

VINCENT, John A. C. 'A Bristol ancestor of the Dukes of Somerset', N.S., 11, 1896, p.73-5. Concerns Mark William, whose daughter Isobel married John Seymour, 1424.

WILLIAMS

SAVARY, A. W. 'Ancestry of General Sir William Fenwick Williams, of Kars, and incidentally a maternal line of the present Marquis of Donegal', N.S., 27, 1911, p.201-13. See also 28, 1912, p.64. 17-19th c.

See also Pointer and Powell

WILLOUGHBY

BODDINGTON, Reginald Stuart. 'Pedigree of the family of Willoughby', 2, 1878, p.91-4. London & Wiltshire; 17th c.

MASSINGBERD, W. O. 'Willoughby of Willoughby, Co. Lincoln', N.S., 18, 1902, p.230-33. 13-14th c.

PINK, W. D. 'The Barony of Willoughby of Parham', 4, 1880, p.34-49. Sussex.

See also Bland and Pointer

WINDE

SMITH, J. Challenor. 'Capt. William Winde, the architect', N.S., 31, 1915, p.243-4. 18th c.

WODE

SMITH, J. Challenor. 'John Wode, Speaker of the House of Commons, 1482-4', N.S., 36, 1920, p.57-61. London & Sussex; includes pedigree, 14-15th c.

WODEHOUSE

RYE, Walter. 'Doubtful Norfolk pedigrees, no. IV: Wodehouse', 3, 1879, p.129-32. 13-14th c.

WOLFE

NORCLIFFE, C. B. 'General James Wolfe at Culloden', 7, 1883, p.225-9. Invernesshire; 18th c.

WOLLEY

M[ARSHALL], G. W. 'Notes on the family of Wolley', 1, 1877, p.118-21. Nottinghamshire & Derbyshire; entries from family bible, with pedigree, 16-17th c.

WOOD

TWIGGE, R. W. 'Pedigree of the family of Wood of Northumberland', 2, 1878, p.201-9. 17-19th c.

WOODS

'In memoriam', N.S., 20, 1904, p.285-6. Sir Albert William Woods.

'Sir Albert William Woods, K.C.M.G., C.B., Garter King of Arms', N.S., 9, 1893, p.241. 19th c.

WORCESTER

See Quincey

WORLYNGTON

SMITH, W. H. 'Evidence as to burial of Sir Hugh Worlyngton, priest of Repynghale, Co. Lincoln', N.S., 11, 1895, p.116-7. 1466.

WRAY

WRAY, George Octavius. 'Family and pedigree of Wray', 4, 1880, p.278-85. See also 5, 1881, p.141-2. Yorkshire; 16-18th c.

WREN

LAW, W. T. 'Note on the Wren pedigree', N.S., 6, 1890, p.168-71.

SMITH, H. Stinton. 'Pedigree of Wren', N.S., 1, 1884, p.262-6. Of various counties; 16-17th c.

WRIGHT

See Maudit

WRIGHTSON

DALLAS, James. 'Family of Wrightson', 3, 1879, p.400-402. Yorkshire; 18th c.

WROTHAM

DERING, Mrs. Cholmeley. 'William de Wrotham, Lord Warden of the Cinque ports', 4, 1880, p.106-8. 12th c.

WROTTESLEY

WROTTESLEY, George. History of the family of Wrottesley of Wrottesley, Co. Stafford. Exeter: W. Pollard & Co., 1903. Supplement to Genealogist, N.S., 15-19.

WEDGWOOD, Josiah C. 'Memoir of Major-General the Hon. George Wrottesley, N.S., 26, 1910, p.40-44.

WYKE

ELLIS, W. S. 'Wyke or Weekes of Kent and Sussex', 1, 1877, p.192-3 & 222-5. See also 2, 1878, p.95-6.1

WYMBERLEY

GREEN, Everard. 'Pedigree of the family of Wymberley of Pinchbeck, Co. Lincoln', 4, 1880, p.6-10. 16-17th c.

WYNANTZ

See Portales

WYTTLEBURY

See Poynton

YOUNGHUSBAND

TWIGGE, R. W. 'Notes on the family of Younghusband of Northumberland', 2, 1878, p.7-13 & 53-64. Includes pedigree, 17-19th c.

AUTHOR INDEX

PLACENAME INDEX